THE CHILDREN'S RIGHTS MOVEMENT

A History of Advocacy and Protection

SOCIAL MOVEMENTS PAST AND PRESENT

Irwin T. Sanders, Editor

THE CHILDREN'S RIGHTS MOVEMENT

A History of
Advocacy and Protection

Joseph M. Hawes

Twayne Publishers ● Boston
A Division of G. K. Hall & Co.

The Children's Rights Movement in the United States
A History of Advocacy and Protection
Joseph M. Hawes

Copyright 1991 by Joseph M. Hawes.
All rights reserved.
Published by Twayne Publishers
A division of G. K. Hall & Co.
70 Lincoln Street
Boston, Massachusetts 02111

Copyediting supervised by Barbara Sutton.
Book production by Janet Z. Reynolds.
Typeset by Compset, Inc. of Beverly, Massachusetts.

First published 1991.
10 9 8 7 6 5 4 3 2 1 (hc)
10 9 8 7 6 5 4 3 2 1 (pb)

Library of Congress Cataloging-in-Publication Data

Hawes, Joseph M.
The children's rights movement of the United States : a history of
advocacy and protection / Joseph M. Hawes.
p.   cm.—(Social movements past and present)
Includes bibliographical references and index.
ISBN 0-8057-9747-5 (hc).—ISBN 0-8057-9748-3 (pbk.)
1. Children's rights—United States—History.   I. Title.
II. Series.
HQ789.H39   1991
305.23—dc20
91-10922

For Gail, whose inspiration and support have made this book possible

Contents

Preface

Although most current members of the children's rights movement believe that they and their cause are relatively new, they are actually part of a long history of efforts to use public power and pressure to improve the lives of American children and thereby to reform or improve American society generally. To understand what today's child advocates and child liberationists are trying to accomplish, their efforts must be seen in a broader historical context. To understand what their struggle is about, it is necessary to describe earlier struggles and the victories and defeats of their predecessors.

Contrary to the teachings of some historians, Americans have a long tradition of being sensitive to the needs and rights of children; but that tradition has competed with others that have sometimes overwhelmed it. The colonists of Massachusetts Bay, seeking to define the legal relationships between parents and children and at the same time send a clear message to large and unruly sons, nevertheless left a small loophole in their "stubborn child" law of 1641. They allowed the child room for self-defense if the parents had been abusive. So limited a provision for the elimination of child abuse seems hardly worth notice to contemporary child advocates, but to have such an exception in the preindustrial world was in itself remarkable.

Other students of the history of child abuse believe that American society only became aware of the problem after C. Henry Kempe's "The Battered Child Syndrome" was published in 1962.[1] But as N. Ray Hiner has shown, Americans had responded to child abuse in an organized and public way in the late nineteenth century, and as John R. Sutton, Elizabeth Pleck, and Linda Gordon have recently shown, efforts to stem family violence and protect children from the evils of both society and their own families are older than the nation itself.[2]

The question of rights for children is a difficult one—particularly in the legal arena. The very notion of rights implies a certain amount of autonomy for the person who exercises them, but children are inherently less than fully autonomous. Indeed, children are not only nonautonomous but, as Michael Grossberg has pointed out, they are "double dependent: on their parents and the state." Thus, a tension exists between the desire to protect children from harm by granting them rights and the recognition that to make children into adults with full autonomy is to deny the reality of their physical and emotional immaturity. This tension has led over the course of American history to a series of conflicts about the nature of children and childhood, as well as conflicts between various public policies of the state and those who have sought to improve the lives of the nation's children.[3]

On one side of these disputes has been a tendency to see the fundamental needs of children as "rights" or entitlements; on the other side is the willingness to grant a greater degree of autonomy to children. Advocates of both views speak of children's rights, but in fact they are pulling in opposite directions. The "protectionists," those who wish to grant children both the right to have their fundamental needs met and a claim on certain kinds of treatment, would protect children from the abuses of adults by citing their right to be free from abuse and asserting that they have the same natural rights to life, liberty, and property as adult citizens. Ironically, perhaps, children's property rights have almost never been in dispute, but the protectionist would be quick to point out that children with significant amounts of property are a distinct, elite minority. Child liberationists, those who would grant more autonomy to children, see the state and parents as the principal oppressors of children. Both kinds of advocates speak in terms of children's rights, and both can claim to be a part of the children's rights movement.

In a sense, the children's rights movement has had to reinvent itself several times. There was a sensitivity to and awareness of children during the colonial period and a surprising amount of discourse about them, but by no stretch of the imagination can a movement on their behalf be discerned. Early in the history of the American Republic, however, there *was* an effort to define the rights of children more precisely and to marshal resources for them. The creation in the nineteenth century of public schools and institutions for all sorts of troubled children indicates both a growing concern about children and a desire to bring both them and society under control. Looking back on that period, we are struck by the heavy hand of these early reformers and their affinity for imposing buildings, strict regulations, and heavy doses of moral invective. To see who the reformers were and what they were trying to do, it is necessary to understand the context in which they worked. At that time there was little disagreement about what children needed, and like the child advocates of today, these early crusaders for juvenile houses of refuge or reform sought to make life better for the children who came their way. To be sure, they were also trying to fix the ills of society, but is not that also one of the unifying characteristics of today's children's rights movement?

Late in the nineteenth century another wave of reform swept the country. Much of the reform attention of the Progressive Era was focused on children and their needs, and more organized campaigns on their behalf were launched at this time. An agency designed to protect children from child abuse was established in the fourth quarter of the nineteenth century, and that effort was supported by the drive for compulsory school attendance laws, the crusade against child labor, and the creation of a new institution, the juvenile court. Progressives believed that they had found the means to reshape society: improve conditions for the children of today and the world of the future will be automatically transformed.

The twentieth century saw the beginnings of a series of regular, national conferences, the White House Conferences on Children and Youth, that assessed the needs of the nation's children and recommended legislation and policies to meet those needs. In the 1920s, as prosperity encouraged consumption and new lifestyles, American youth blossomed and became a national obsession. The rise of the peer group marked a turning point in the relationship between children and the larger society and raised, if it did not answer, the question of how much the ideas and opinions of children themselves ought to be considered by child savers and advocates. Also in the 1920s the nation saw its infant mortality rate decline as a result of the successful federal programs set up by the Sheppard-Towner Act, which provided for health education and prenatal care.

Before the question of the role of children and youth in social policies could be more thoroughly addressed, the nation fell into the depths of the Great Depression of the 1930s. But at that time the nation could at least focus on and address children's basic necessities. Out of this concern came the country's largest welfare program, Aid to Dependent Children, which was sponsored by a government agency, the U.S. Children's Bureau.

During World War II the Children's Bureau pioneered in the development of special medical care for the families of servicemen, and through the provisions of the Lanham Act, the government provided assistance for the creation of day-care centers to aid defense production. When the war ended, however, so did these actions in aid of children and their families, and the nation began to worry more about juvenile delinquency and youth gangs than it did about children's needs and rights.

In the 1960s the nation began to look again at the needs of children. At a time when the civil rights movement was in full swing and many middle-class women, the traditional advocates of children's interests, came to see themselves as an oppressed group, the Children's Bureau, the Child Welfare League, social workers, teachers, day-care workers, parents' organizations, and so on, saw the need for organized campaigns if any changes in the way the United States treated its children were to be made. The modern children's rights movement was born, and its members would attract public attention, influence the course of legislation, and, when necessary, file litigation to see that children's rights were acknowledged and enforced.

Because of its complexity (and indeed, because of some of its contradictions), the children's rights movement is best understood in historical terms. The method of this book is to trace the evolution of ideas and practices central to the movement from colonial times to the present. The methods of the historian are eclectic: "survivals," both documents and artifacts, do not conform to contemporary notions of what we would like to know. But the historian must work with what has survived, which is always far less than he or she would wish. In the pages that follow I have sought to provide a coherent account of changing sensibilities about children and their rights from the colonial period to the present.

The fond hope of historians is that their work will make a difference. Perhaps this brief overview of the children's rights movement will enable future advocates to avoid reinventing the idea of a crusade on behalf of children. There is an honorable history here—a tradition that today's activists can use as they continue their efforts.

Acknowledgments

Thanks are due to many different people for their help on this project. I owe a considerable debt to Irwin Sanders, who first suggested the idea for this book. To those at Twayne who have worked with me, Athanaide Dallet and John Martin, I also express my sincere thanks for their patience and help. I wish to acknowledge the support of Memphis State University, especially the Department of History. The university provided released time from teaching, and the department provided secretarial and other forms of support. Also important for this work was the Interlibrary Loan Department of Brister Library, especially Deborah Brackstone; of essential assistance to the project was the library's online search capability. I am also grateful to the law and education libraries of Vanderbilt University for permission to use their superb collections and facilities. Finally, thanks to Edwin Frank and Michelle Fagan of the Mississippi Valley Collection and to Constance Shulz of the University of South Carolina for their assistance in obtaining photographs.

Chapter One

Parens Patriae and the Foundation of Child Protection Laws, 1640–1800

The primary social institution in the colonial period of American history was the family. The family was, in effect, a comprehensive, organic unit, "a little Church, and a little commonwealth, at least a lively representation thereof, whereby triall may be made of such as are fit for any place of authoritie, or of subjection in Church or commonwealth. Or rather it is a schoole wherein men are fitted to greater matters in Church or commonwealth."[1]

Children had rights in the colonial period—or to put it in the terms of that period, they had a recognized status that entitled them to such things as the necessities of life, a start in life, and freedom from excessive abuse. Children, like everyone else in the colonial world, had a place in it and were punished if they failed to keep their place.

Although some historians have argued that during the colonial period children were regarded as miniature adults, a remarkable amount of attention was focused on them. Colonists recognized some of the developmental issues of today and had a rudimentary concept of adolescence. But the principal difference between them and modern adults is that they rarely thought about children as individuals. In addition, they had none of the children's social agencies and institutions that are so much a part of contemporary society.

The web of relationships, both legal and customary, in the lives of colonial children was perhaps best summed up in the common law, according to which the duties of parents included "maintaining and educating them during the season of infancy and youth" and giving them a start in life, that is, "making reasonable provision for their future usefulness and happiness in life." Under the common law, "the father (and on his death the mother) is generally entitled to the custody of the infant children," because the parents are the children's "natural protectors." Nevertheless, "when the morals, or safety, or interests of the children require it," the courts could intervene and "withdraw the infants from the custody of the father or mother and place the care and custody of them elsewhere."[2] This power to intervene, on behalf of the child, even in the biological family, stems from the doctrine of *parens patriae:* the state is the ultimate parent of every child.

The social world during much of the colonial period operated in what twentieth-century Americans would consider an intrusive manner. The boundaries between families and communities were quite permeable, and as a result, the privacy of the family was almost nonexistent. People minded each other's business, but in doing so protected the dependent members of households from excessive abuse. Also contributing to the relative lack of abuse of children, women, and servants was the economy of the colonial period. Relatively few families accumulated enough wealth to enjoy any sort of leisure. Except for a few artisans (and later, manufacturing workers and tradespeople in the cities), almost everyone was a farmer. Most farmers had to work continuously simply to survive. The constant struggle left little room for disputes or disagreements.

Society in the colonial period was carefully structured and held "a place for everyone and everyone in his or her place." Relationships between people were seen in terms of mutual obligations. Those of lesser rank were obliged to defer to their betters and carried titles in accord with their station. "We must bear one another's burthens," John Winthrop said in a sermon on the *Arabella* as it made its way across the Atlantic, but he cautioned his listeners not to expect any change in social status once they reached the new world.

Children in New England

The colonists at Plymouth and in the larger Massachusetts Bay Colony regarded society as a collection of families rather than individuals. To them the notion of individual rights would have seemed strange indeed, largely because they saw isolated individuals as dangerous to the peace of society. Strangers could be warned away from a New England colony or required to live with a family.

Families were not only social but economic units in which members worked cooperatively for their mutual survival. Families produced almost everything they consumed and rarely had much in the way of a surplus. Husbands, sons, and male servants worked in the fields clearing, plowing, planting, cultivating, and harvesting. When they were not so engaged they built fences, tended livestock, repaired tools and equipment, and so on. In the house or close by, women, daughters, and female servants kept kitchen gardens, did all the cooking, and made the clothing from scratch, as well as all the other necessities of life, such as soap, candles, beer, and the like.

Children were very much a part of this world and became productive members of it as soon as they were capable (typically around age seven). They "earned their keep" by helping out in the myriad tasks of the preindustrial household. Sons worked beside fathers and learned the skills necessary to function as adult males in that world. Daughters similarly worked beside their mothers. Child care, such as it was, belonged to the female members of the household, but education, especially moral education, was the responsibility of the husband/father.

In its government, the family truly was "a little commonwealth." The husband/father presided over the family like a patriarch, although John Demos argues that much of the decision-making in the family involved both the husband and the wife.[3] Wives were clearly subordinate to husbands and were legally nonexistent so far as making contracts was concerned. Children fell somewhere below parents; their relationship to the servants of the household is not clear.

According to John Demos, the relationship between parents and children could be conceived of as a set of mutual obligations. Children obeyed their parents, just as the Bible commanded them to "honor thy father and mother." Parents were obliged to meet the child's basic needs and to provide education in the broadest sense, as well as the means whereby the child could eventually leave home and become an adult. Typically, this last obligation was discharged by providing the child with his or her "portion" of property, either to make a living from if a son or to set up housekeeping with if a daughter.

The education of children in Puritan New England took place in a variety of contexts and often as a part of ordinary life. While formal schools existed in colonial America and became more common in the late eighteenth century, according to John Demos, "they formed a kind of appendage to other far more important, comprehensive agencies: the church, the community at large, and above all, the family itself."[4]

The values New Englanders sought to implant in their children were primarily negative. According to James Axtell, parents in New England sought to tame children's natural tendencies to be "disobedient, stubborn, untractable, independent, contentious, insubordinate, rebellious, unwieldy, inflexible, obstinate, and proud." Consequently, Axtell notes, "New England primarily educated its children, not toward an ideal of human nature, but away from a postlapsarian Adamic character."[5] Such a view flowed naturally from the doctrine of infant depravity, which held that children were born in sin and, to become regenerate, Christian adults, had to be born again. Children who died before they were baptized were necessarily condemned to hell, though as one Puritan put it, they would be assigned to the "easiest room in hell." Such an uncompromising view, though technically correct, won few adherents among the ordinary folk of colonial New England. As the historian Peter Slater has argued, "Puritan mothers and fathers did not see vessels of sin and depravity every time they glanced at one of their infants." Slater indicates that the Puritans saw children as a paradox—"an innocent facade behind which lurked all sorts of wicked desires."[6]

To ensure that children understood their place, New England's two most prominent educational theorists, Rev. John Robinson, minister to the congregation of the Pilgrims in Holland, and Rev. Cotton Mather, son of the towering Increase and the namesake of John Cotton, both recommended threatening children with eternal damnation to make them conform. "Disobedient Children! my heart aches for you," Mather wrote, "for I have seen the judgments of God making such as you the most astonishing monuments of his indignation." Robinson said simply, "The Lord affords long life to such as 'honor father and mother.'"[7]

Thus, colonial New England looked upon its children with a suspicious eye, ready to catch the slightest slip from orthodoxy or due deference. So great was the concern with propriety and with the use of threats as a means of breaking the will of children that the *Body of Liberties,* enacted in 1641, included a provision that made the cursing and striking of parents a capital crime: "If any child, or children, above sixteen years old, and of sufficient understanding, shall CURSE or SMITE their natural FATHER, or MOTHER, he or she shall be putt to death, unless it can be sufficiently testifyed that the Parents have been very unchristianly negligent in the education of such children: so provoked them by extreme and cruel correction, that they have been forced thereunto, to preserve themselves from death or maiming." In 1646 the Massachusetts General Court added the following:

If a man have a stubborn or rebellious son, of sufficient years and understanding (viz.) sixteen years of age, which will not obey the voice of his Father, or the voice of his Mother, and that when they have chastened him will not hearken unto them: then shall his Father and Mother being his natural parents, lay hold on him, and bring him to the Magistrates assembled in Court and testify unto them, that their son is stubborn and rebellious and will not obey their voice and chastisement, but lives in sundry notorious crimes, such a son shall be put to death.[8]

The first law, taken primarily from English law, not only provided for the punishment of fractious children but also gave them the opportunity to argue that they had been abused or that they had acted in self-defense. The second version, the so-called stubborn child law, which broadened the definition of rebellious children, did not include this allowance; but it did require the appearance of the stubborn son before the court. The *Body of Liberties* also included a provision that "everie marryed woeman shall be free from bodilie correction or stripes by her husband, unless it be in his owne defence upon her assault." Similarly, the *Body of Liberties* forbade parents from choosing their child's mate (a practice more honored in the breach) and also admonished parents to avoid "unnatural severitie" toward their children. The *Body of Liberties* granted children "free libertie to complain to the Authorities for redresse."[9]

This set of laws was the first code anywhere in the world to offer legal protection of any kind to children (and to wives, for that matter). The laws point in two seemingly contradictory directions: they afford children some protection from abuse (or at least, "unnatural severitie"), but at the same time they add the power of the state to parental authority. In time, that state power would become the means whereby society intervened in families on behalf of the children.

The *ideas* expressed in these laws seem to contain the seeds of the modern concern with individual rights, including children's rights. At the time, the laws seem not to have had much effect: no young people were ever put to death under the provisons of the stubborn child law, and there were no cases of children winning against their parents in court. Nevertheless, the state had a strong tendency to supervise family life while administering justice. The following case, taken from the records of the Suffolk County Court in 1673, illustrates the importance of the relationship between the court and the parents:

John Chandler and Elizabeth Chandler Son & daughter of John Chandler senr of Roxbury being presented to this Court for wanton uncivill & unseemly carriages

The Court upon learning of the case, what was proved & what was owned by themselves doe Sentence the sd John & Elizabeth to bee severely whip't by theire Father & mother in theire own house in presence of the Constable & John Stebbins. The father to correct his Son & the mother her daughter with such a Number of stripes as the Constable & sd Stebbins shall judge meete not exceeding fifteen stripes apiece & that the sd children bee put asunder & not suffered to dwell together till the Court take further order.[10]

This case illustrates that the court not only provided the constable and another witness to oversee the punishment, but that it also ordered the children to be separated until it saw fit to allow them to be together again. Thus, the case also illustrates the ability of the state to intervene directly in family life, as it saw fit.

A complicating factor in the study of the rights of children in the colonial period is that many of them did not live or grow up in their own households. The practice of placing out children has intrigued contemporary historians for some time. The venerable historian of the Puritan family, Edmund S. Morgan, believed that Puritans placed their children out because they were afraid of loving them too much.[11] Recently, however, Ross Beales has suggested that "the number and sex composition of a family's children may have encouraged parents to place some of them in other households." The receiving households may have sought to add some children in order to gain additional hands to help with the work: girls for child care and housework, boys to work in the fields.[12] Thus, many of the children in colonial America spent a substantial portion of their time as servants in a family other than their own. We might say today that a good many children were placed in foster homes—but with their parents' consent and assistance. Virginia passed a statute in 1646 enabling the local authorities to actually undertake this "binding out" themselves:

Whereas sundry laws and statutes by act of parliament established, have with great wisdom ordained for the better educating of youth in honest and profitable trades and manufactures, as also to avoyd sloath and idlenesse wherewith such young children are easily corrupted. As also for releife of such parents whose poverty extends not to give them breeding, That the justices of the peace should at their discretion, bind out children to tradesmen or husbandmen to be brought up in some good and lawfull calling.[13]

In the colonial world the concept of *parens patriae* was so pervasive that it scarcely received comment. In both Massachusetts and Virginia there was no challenge to the state's assumption of authority over the internal workings of the family. Not only was the state the ultimate parent of the child, the state claimed moral and religious authority as well.

In the eighteenth century, after the glory days of Puritanism, the moral authority of the state remained. The selectmen of Watertown, Massachusetts, after hearing complaints about families that were "under very neady & suffering circumstances," resolved on 24 March 1737 that the town clerk would post a notice to inform the families that they should "take care to put out and dispose of their children to such families where they may be taken good care of." The selectmen believed that the families in question had been guilty of "negligence and indulgence" and had brought up their children in "idleness, ignorance, and ereligion [*sic*]." The selectmen justified their actions on the grounds that they were "willing to do their duty" and that "the law expects . . . them to present such mischiefs." If the parents failed to place their children out, the selectmen were prepared to "take effectual care that such children be forthwith put into such families where they may have good care taken of them."[14]

Taking Care of Orphans

Orphans presented a special case. Nowhere was their plight more acute in the colonial period than on the tobacco plantations of the Chesapeake region; the death rate was terrible there in the seventeenth century owing to malaria. The plantations required intensive labor, which created a demand for indentured servants (and later, slaves), some of whom were single women who had migrated to the Chesapeake in search of fortunes or a new start in life. Family life was extremely unstable, and as a result, the most elaborate and systematic way of dealing with orphans developed in the Chesapeake.[15] The legal mechanisms in use in Maryland in the seventeenth century were the probate court and the county orphan's courts. When a man died without leaving a will, the courts would appoint a guardian to look after the interests of his children. Bond was required, but mothers and stepfathers could be named guardians without it until 1696. After that date, the courts enforced the requirements for sureties and would remove children from their mothers or stepfathers when the guarantees could not be found. After children reached the age of 14, they could choose their own guardians. The court assigned orphans with little or no property to families, with the understanding that the children would work for their keep. The courts were supposed to check on the welfare of orphans under their supervision; in 1681 Maryland passed a law that called for the empaneling of special juries to check on the welfare of orphans.

The system for orphans whose fathers had died intestate worked so well that in 1696 the Maryland legislature extended the jurisdiction of the orphan's courts to all orphans and gave the courts the power to remove children from families or guardians despite the provisions of a will. Thus, the colony of Maryland recognized that children had interests of their own, and it provided a system that would guarantee children's rights— at least their rights to a certain amount of property and the right to be free from abuse. The colony created special courts and a special jury system to protect those rights, ample testimony to the importance accorded children's interests.[16]

In colonial New England the same set of circumstances did not lead to the placement of children with foster families. Instead, the courts placed children with their nearest blood relative. The difference between the practices of the two areas resulted from the extraordinarily high death rate in Maryland, which in turn frequently disrupted families and made the more elaborate institutional arrangements necessary.[17] But the practice in both areas was to protect the interests of children, to make sure that the property that was rightfully theirs remained intact and passed into their hands on maturity. The state thus oversaw the delicate process of passing property between generations and acted to guarantee what may be described as children's rights. The power to do this rested in English tradition, which also allowed children over 14 a voice in their own cause. Of course, the point of this solicitude was to ensure that children had the necessary means to make a start in life so that they would not become paupers and public charges.

In addition to the practice of binding out, colonial America also saw the creation of the orphanage, the earliest of which was established in 1729 at the Ursuline Convent in New Orleans. An orphanage in Georgia, Bethesda, became well known because it was the special project of the famous evangelist George Whitfield. Whitfield argued that orphanages were more humane than the system of vendue, under which local authorities literally auctioned off children and other dependents to the lowest acceptable bidder. A passage from his journal reflects his views:

Tuesday, Jan. 29 [1740]. Took in three German orphans, the most pitiable objects I think I ever saw. . . . They have been used to exceeding hard labour, and though supplied with provisions from the trustees, were treated in a manner unbecoming even heathens. Were all the money I have collected, to be spent in freeing these children from slavery, it would be well laid out. I have also in my house near twenty more, who, in all probability, if not taken in, would be as ignorant of God and Christ as the Indians.[18]

There was trouble at Bethesda after Whitfield left. The local authorities took some of the children away from the orphanage and bound them out, and some orphans ran away. One runaway came to the notice of the secretary of the colony, Col. William Stephens:

June 16, 1741. Complaint being made to Bailiff Parker, that one of the Orphan Boys, under the care of Mr. Whitfield, had been treated with unwarrantable Correction, by Mr. Barber the Presbyterian minister there, he was summoned to appear at Savannah, by Warrant to the Constable. . . . The Boy who had suffered (it seems) had run away to Mr. Parker for protection, at his Plantation at the Isle of Hope; where Parker being not well at that Time, had delay'd coming to Town for near a fortnight, to have it enquir'd into; by which Means the stripes he had seen fresh upon the Boy, did not now appear so terrible as at first: However, the Boy being now present, and stripp'd, it is yet too visible from Scars and Wounds not yet healed, that great Cruelty had been used; It was not denied that the Boy was made naked to the Waist, after the manner of common Malefactors, and lashed with five strong Twigs tied together, as long as they would hold, whereby his whole Back, Shoulders, Loins, Flank, and Belly, were in a dreadful Condition.[19]

The severity of this beating reminds us that while the state did intervene in family life and provide mechanisms whereby children would not starve, society at that time had a very different conception of the nature of child abuse. The legal framework was in place to assert some idea of children's rights, and the authorities sometimes used their power, but in ordinary daily life hardly anyone thought much about children's rights. When society did respond to children's needs, it did so on an individual basis, as in the case above. But it can be argued that even when children benefited most from the intervention of the state, the goal of that intervention was not to protect children from abuse but to reduce the drain on the public treasury and to maintain social order and stability.

Conclusion

The colonial period abounds in ironies where children are concerned. There was no clear conception of children's rights, but the first law that contained an idea that children had a claim to self-preservation, protection, and a future of their own appeared in colonial America. The Puritans, whose image as stern oppressors has persisted in spite of the best efforts of several generations of historians, laid the foundation for the child protection laws enacted in the nineteenth and twentieth centuries; they also developed and applied the concept of *parens patriae,* which is the legal basis for all state intervention on behalf of children today. Other achievements of this era were the passage of the first stubborn child law and the development of a special-purpose institution for children, the orphanage.

As the period ended with the birth of a new republic, children had what we may label rights. They had a right to a start in life, a right to life itself, and a right to be free from unusual severity in the punishment they might receive from parent or guardian. If the children lacked a parent or guardian, the state supervised their property in the place of the parent. At the center of all this was the family; it was the institution that did all welfare work. Local authorities depended on families to do this work. In the nineteenth century, society developed institutions to supplement the work of the family, but the state's authority derived from *parens patriae* would continue.

Chapter Two

The Age of Institution Building, 1800–1890

If the colonial period saw the passage of the first stubborn child law and the enactment of the idea that children deserve protection from abuse, the nineteenth century saw a number of social efforts designed to improve children's lives and, in some cases, to protect their rights. The Puritan notion of infant depravity was expanded upon by nineteenth-century reformers, who saw children as both needing redemption and being capable of redeeming society.

The ideas of the English philosopher John Locke provided a handy counterpart to the grim doctrine of original sin. Most Puritan ministers, following the lead of Jonathan Edwards, accepted the outlines of John Locke's *Essay Concerning Human Understanding.* But, like Edwards, they applied the idea that a child was a tabula rasa at birth to the child's rational faculties alone. In time, the distinction became blurred, and those who read Locke began to view a child's psyche, as well as his or her reason, as blank or neutral at birth. In effect, the Enlightenment triumphed over original sin by emphasizing the primacy of environmental influences in shaping individual character and conscience.[1]

Children therefore deserved to be saved from the evils of an industrializing society, but they also represented the future and the possibilities of a better life. Thus, Americans built schools to provide a disciplined and literate work force and to give poor children a chance to improve their lives. Americans also built special institutions for those children already in difficulty in the hope that children might be "re-formed."

An emphasis on environment formed an important part of the complex of ideas behind the institutions created in the early nineteenth century for children. The founders of those institutions believed that they could alter the character of young people by providing the proper environment. Houses of refuge stressed order and discipline. According to the historian David Rothman, "At the core of the child-reformers' optimism was a faith completely shared by colleagues promoting other caretaker institutions that a daily routine of strict and steady discipline would transform inmates' character."[2]

But the Enlightenment emphasis on reason and environmental influences gave way to a new movement, reflected in both the reform and child-rearing advice literature. The rise of romanticism gave American society yet another image of children's inner natures. Puritans saw children as innately sinful; Lockeans saw them as neutral; romantics regarded children as innately good—even morally superior to adults. The rise of romanticism in the United States had important consequences for the growth and development of children's rights. By contributing to the sentimentalization of children, romantics gave child advocates the tool they needed to rouse public opinion on behalf of the child.[3]

Nineteenth-century Americans sought to indoctrinate all children with the values of rugged individualism—especially those children whose lives already demonstrated that they could and did support themselves. Thus, Americans held contradictory views of children in the nineteenth century. On the one hand, they expected children to save society by virtue of their innocence, while on the other, Horatio Alger harangued millions with his stories of economic success won by dint of hard work, a good character, and a final stroke of luck.

As if these two images were not contradictory enough, society also saw poor children—particularly those who lived by their wits on the streets—as dangerous. The emerging ethos of individualism in nineteenth-century America contained a strong element of self-reliance, which in turn implied a strong degree of self-discipline. Children loose on the streets, who were referred to as "street Arabs," seemed to be begging for someone to step in and take charge. The principal response to this challenge was the creation of a variety of schools and programs designed, almost literally, to get the kids off the streets.

The problem of the conflicting images of children in the nineteenth century resolves itself into an issue of class. When American society became republican, it lost a sense of hierarchy and deference. As a result, it had to start relying on *individual* conformity to the moral code in order to preserve the social order. How to develop this conformity? The answer was the institution of "republican motherhood": middle-class mothers, now entrusted with both the care and the education of their children, would inculcate the civic virtues into the hearts of their children (daughters as well as sons, for they were future mothers and thus trainers of generations yet unborn). Thus, middle-class children would save society by providing it with virtuous leadership; but lower-class children carousing in the streets far from the influence of a republican mother threatened society.

In many respects, the modern concept of children's rights seems far removed from the efforts to get children off the streets and the idealism of republican motherhood. Nevertheless, there were threads of the idea of rights in all of these developments. Children might claim a right to an education or the right to separate incarceration if found guilty of a crime—or even possibly, the right to reformation. We can also see the beginnings of the concepts of social and psychological rights as society began to pay attention to motherhood. Nineteenth-century institution building did not do much to expand the rights of children, but it did illustrate how the state could exercise its enormous powers under *parens patriae* and intervene directly in the lives of children, a practice that intensified in this period and has been expanding ever since.

A major development in the area of children's rights in the nineteenth century was the founding in 1875 of the Society for the Prevention of Cruelty to Children (SPCC), which was the first specific, formal response to the question of child abuse and child neglect. Besides directing attention to the problem of child abuse, "the Cruelty," as the SPCC was called in immigrant neighborhoods, helped to refine the concept of abuse. The idea already laid down in the colonial period—that children have the right to live and grow and that society, usually through the agency of the family, has the duty to preserve that right—expanded into the notion that a quasi-public agency could intervene to protect a child from abuse and neglect.

Public Schools

Undoubtedly the most important institution created for children in the early nineteenth century was the common school. These schools appeared in response to public concern about an industrializing, urbanizing, expanding free society. According to the editors of *Children and Youth in America,* the concerted effort to create public schools was "an attempt to secure a common core of belief and loyalty in order to maintain a balance between social stability and liberty." The schools had two missions: they "were expected to mold the young into loyal and useful American citizens," as well as "to assist the young in developing and fulfilling their capabilities, helping them to unlock the potentials of mind and character that would free them from error and narrowness."[4] Children were supposed to learn how to succeed and then rise through the ranks. Education was to be the cure for the danger from the lower classes.

The creation of public schools, reformers argued, would solve the social ills of American society. And those ills were mounting rapidly. Religion was in decline; gone forever were the days of Puritan ascendancy when the family could be counted on to enforce the moral code of society. In fact, the family that could do that was gone, too. The patriarchal father of the preindustrial family was responsible for the moral education of his children, and if they misbehaved, the community would hold him accountable. But in the newly rising cities like Boston, New York, and Philadelphia he was no longer at home or nearby during the day. Fathers went out to work, and moral education was left to mothers. With religion no longer salient in Americans' lives (or at least, so said the evangelists who preached the second coming), something had to be done, and quickly.

The answer was to create a system of public schools for all children, well-to-do and poor alike. The schools would replace churches and families and emphasize moral instruction as well as practical information. Thus, educators in Boston and New England between 1820 and 1860 came to see the common school as a "community in miniature" created specifically for children. According to Stanley Schulz, "The teacher could stand in place of the parent, examining the character, morals and habits of each child, and exercising the moral authority that had once belonged exclusively to the family." Consequently, the public school was to be "a classroom, a family room, a church house—all things to all children."[5]

The idea of public schools was not new in the early nineteenth century, but reformers like Horace Mann urged that the public schools be for all children, not just for the children of the poor. The new model public schools would thus avoid the stigma of being "charity schools" and would be of higher quality if they attracted the children of the better classes.

The schools thus created were not, as it turned out, the free, universally attended public schools of the twentieth century. In the first place, attendance was voluntary, and in the second, there were never enough schools to meet the demand for them. A third problem surfaced when it became clear that many of the children enticed into the public schools lacked the skills necessary to compete with better-prepared children. The school leaders tried two kinds of compensatory education: the monitorial system, whereby older children taught younger ones, and special schools for those unable to meet the standards of the regular schools. Neither worked too well. With the great influx of immigrants in the 1850s, schools in large cities were overwhelmed—they were overcrowded and seemingly ineffectual.[6]

Houses of Refuge

Early on in the campaign to develop public schools, some authorities focused on the need to develop a special kind of institution for youthful lawbreakers. Those young people who had missed out on the opportunities the public schools provided or whose background had deprived them of an adequate moral education needed special attention. In three cities, New York, Boston, and Philadelphia, earnest urban reformers dealt with this special class of children by creating a new institution, the "house of refuge." Believing that youthful characters could be remolded, the founders of refuges stressed rigorous discipline, education, and work as the principal means of reformation.

In 1823 the Society for the Prevention of Pauperism in the City of New York called a public meeting for the discussion of its annual report, which called for the creation of a house of refuge for juvenile delinquents. The society renamed itself the Society for the Reformation of Juvenile Delinquents and began the campaign that resulted in the creation in 1825 of the first institution for juvenile delinquents in the United States, the New York House of Refuge. The refuge would offer its inmates "such employments as will tend to encourage industry," basic education in "reading, writing, and arithmetic," and instruction in "the nature of their moral and religious obligations." It is worth noting that houses of refuge had separate departments for girls and blacks. The founders of the New York House of Refuge thought that having a separate department for girls would serve those unfortunate young women who were "either too young to have acquired habits of fixed depravity, or those whose lives have in general been virtuous, but who, having yielded to the seductive influence of corrupt associates, have suddenly to endure the bitterness of lost reputation, and are cast forlorn and destitute upon a cold and unfeeling public."[7]

The daily workings of the institution did not meet the founders' ideals. The superintendent contracted with outside businesses for the work of the inmates and agreed to maintain discipline. The original idea was for the inmates to learn a trade and thus support themselves. But the contractors used assembly-line methods that only prepared the inmates for similar dead-end work outside.

Within three years after the opening of the New York House of Refuge, two other similar institutions were founded—the House of Reformation in Boston and the Philadelphia House of Refuge. All three institutions had similar charters, which gave them jurisdiction over criminal and vagrant children. In addition, noncriminal children who appeared to be in need of stern discipline or other aspects of the regime in a refuge could also be committed to the Boston House of Reformation. The institution was supposed to take in "all such children who shall be convicted of criminal offences or taken up and committed under and by virtue of an act of this Commonwealth, 'for suppressing and punishing of rogues, vagabonds, common beggars, and other idle, disorderly and lewd persons.'" The mayor, aldermen, or overseers of the poor could recommend that "all children who live an idle or dissolute life, whose parents are dead, or if living, from drunkenness, or other vices, neglect to provide any suitable employment, or exercise any salutary control over said children," be sentenced to the House of Reformation, where they were to "be kept governed and disposed of, as hereinafter provided, the males till they are of the age of twenty-one years, and the females of eighteen years."[8]

Clearly, the jurisdiction of a house of refuge was broad indeed, since children could be confined until their majority on the basis of crime, vagrancy, the need of discipline, or parental neglect. Using the power of *parens patriae,* the state had greatly extended its control over disorderly and dependent children. On the one hand, this could be seen as an advance for children's rights, since the state was intervening on their behalf and providing, in the case of neglected children, the kind of start in life that was every child's birthright. Children may have lost some rights, however, as the state extended its jurisdiction over misbehaving children. The idea that almost any official could have a child committed for almost any reason meant that children had fewer legal rights than adults.

The question of the legality of the house of refuge came before the courts in 1831 in the case of *Commonwealth* v. *M'Keagy.* Lewis L. Joseph had been committed to the Philadelphia House of Refuge as "an idle and disorderly person," on evidence supplied by his father. What triggered the case was a plea for a writ of habeas corpus. The Court of Common Pleas in Philadelphia ordered Joseph released on the grounds that he was not a vagrant, nor was his father a pauper. In giving its opinion, the court did note approvingly, the novelty of the powers assumed by the refuge, but it also raised the question of the vagueness of the refuge's charter when vagrancy or idleness was at issue: "It is when the law is attempted to be applied to subjects who are not vagrants in the just and legal acceptation of the term; [when] preservation becomes mixed with a punitory character, that doubts are started and difficulties arise, which often involve the most solemn questions of individual and constitutional rights."[9]

In *Commonwealth* v. *M'Keagy,* the court did not consider the issue of the constitutionality of the statute creating the Philadelphia House of Refuge. That challenge appeared in the case of *Ex parte Crouse,* heard by the Pennsylvania Supreme Court in 1839. Like Lewis Joseph, Mary Ann Crouse sought a writ of habeas corpus, but the court denied it, upholding the constitutionality of the refuge. The court ruled that the Philadelphia House of Refuge was not a prison but a school, and concluded, "The infant has been snatched from a course which must have ended in confirmed depravity, and not only is the restraint of her person lawful, but it would be an act of extreme cruelty to release her from it."[10]

The early idealism of the refuge movement was contagious, and the refuge idea spread across the country during the nineteenth century. The most important impact of the refuges was not any alleviation of crime and poverty, as the founders had hoped for, but rather their contribution to an extraordinary expansion of state power. Reformers, judges, and managers of houses of refuge believed that such power was necessary and that its effect was essentially benevolent. After all, they might have argued, the power of *parens patriae* was being used on behalf of the child.

The Children's Aid Society

By the middle of the nineteenth century, the city of New York was a sprawling metropolis with great extremes of wealth and poverty. Newspaper accounts of homeless people were routine, and overcrowding was the norm. When Charles Dickens visited the notorious Five Points District in 1842, he noted that "such lives as are led here, bear the same fruits here as elsewhere. . . . Nearly every house is a low tavern. . . . All that is loathsome, drooping and decayed is here."[11] The death rate soared under such conditions, and when cholera raced through the city in 1849, people died by the thousands.

A new generation of reformers appeared in the 1840s and 1850s: Robert Hartley, the leader of the New York Association for Improving the Condition of the Poor, Charles Loring Brace, who founded the New York Children's Aid Society (CAS), and Rev. Louis Pease, who conducted the Five Points House of Industry. According to Christine Stansell, these new activists rejected the familiar categories of pietism—virtue and vice—and focused on "a surveillance of the material conditions of city life." Thus, they examined "public health, mortality rates and housing conditions." What was new about this approach was their recognition of the environment as a significant factor in the growth of pauperism. What they developed in effect was "a pietistic science of poverty."

This group of reformers believed that the new great city contained the seeds of a terrible crisis, and they sought, through their analysis and programs, to stave off what they regarded as an unthinkable future. They concluded that the people who lived in the crowded slums were the forces of darkness. At first, they focused on tenements and regarded that crowded environment as the source of urban distress. They invented a new concept, the "tenement classes"—a group the reformer Charles Loring Brace would later call the "Perishing and Dangerous Classes." "With the invention of the tenement classes," Stansell notes, "the distinctions between people and their surroundings began to blur, and humanitarian sentiment faded away."[12]

In October 1849 the chief of police of New York City, George W. Matsell, issued a report on the vagrant children on the streets of the city. Matsell referred to the "constantly increasing numbers of vagrant, idle and vicious children." He estimated that there were about 3,000 such children and added that "each year makes fearful additions to the ranks of these prospective recruits of infamy and sin. . . . From this corrupt and festering fountain [Matsell disdained the notion of impartiality] flows a ceaseless stream to our lowest brothels—to the Penitentiary and the State Prison."[13]

One of the responses to the conditions Matsell and others described was the creation of the New York Children's Aid Society in 1853. In a circular announcing its intentions, the CAS declared that it had been created to do something about the problem of children's crime in the city. It would establish an industrial school to provide vocational training, and it would find jobs for idle boys and homes in the country with farmers for the homeless. To this list of programs the society added in 1854 the Newsboys Lodging House, where newsboys got not charity but a bargain: the charge for lodging was a mere 6¢.[14]

According to Stansell, the great numbers of children on the streets that so concerned Chief Matsell were attributable to the increase in street trades. Children who formerly worked as apprentices now found themselves hustling on city streets. Another factor was the difference in class perceptions about the proper activities of children. Urban middle-class families believed that children should be either in school or at home under the tutelage of their mother. Working-class families, by contrast, relied on their children, much as preindustrial families had done, to earn part of the livelihood of the family. They could not afford to let a child go to school and thereby forgo the lost income.[15]

To Brace and other like-minded middle-class reformers, the existence of an army of "street Arabs" was testimony enough to the instability of family life among the working (soon to be "dangerous") classes. To restore the lost family and reclaim a young person on the verge of being lost, Brace and the CAS placed children with farm families in rural areas, where there was still a demand for labor. Brace and his agents combed the city for suitable candidates for their placing-out system; when they could not find orphans, they placed out children whose parents were still living.[16]

The placing-out system developed by the New York Children's Aid Society was a significant precursor to today's welfare system and to the contemporary notion of children's rights. Brace believed that he was acting in the interest of the children he placed out, and he justified the placing of children who were not orphans on the grounds that it would surely be good for them.[17] For the first time a prominent reformer was explicitly placing the interests of the child ahead of those of the family of origin. This would be an essential ingredient in the whole question of children's rights.

The CAS gave different kinds of help to boys and girls. In general, only boys were placed out; girls were enrolled in industrial school (to teach them sewing) and put in lodging houses (to save them from the proverbial fate worse than death).

In 1853 the city of New York passed a school truancy law. The result of the agitations of the New York Association for Improving the Condition of the Poor, the law provided that a family could not receive relief unless its children were in school. The law almost literally banned children from the street and provided that orphans found on the streets could become wards of the state. If children were found to be "habitual wanderers," the state could sever parental rights. Like Brace's placing-out system, this law reflected a growing distrust of working-class families; at the same time, however, it represented an increasing interest in the needs of children. Protecting children from the evils of life on the streets—from life as free and autonomous beings—would come to be called an effort on behalf of children's rights. Ironically, in the late twentieth century some children's rights advocates would seek to restore a similar kind of autonomy.[18]

The Society for the Prevention of Cruelty to Children

If the Children's Aid Society was the middle-class answer to the problem of lower-class children on city streets, the Society for the Prevention of Cruelty to Children was the upper-class answer to the problem of child abuse within families. To be sure, the CAS sometimes placed out children from homes that were intact, but it justified doing so as an effort to get children off the streets. The new agency, on the other hand, proposed to protect children inside their homes and within their families.

The story of the creation of the New York SPCC is familiar to those in the children's rights field. A volunteer social worker (the wife of a very prominent businessman) found that there was no agency willing to intervene on behalf of a neglected and abused 10-year-old girl who was living with her stepmother. In desperation, the social worker turned to Henry Bergh of the Society for the Prevention of Cruelty to Animals (SPCA), who arranged to have the child brought to court. The judge placed the child in the temporary care of the SPCA, which arranged for a foster home. With the help of the SPCA's general counsel, Elbridge Gerry, a new organization, the Society for the Prevention of Cruelty to Children, was founded in 1875.[19]

The New York SPCC appealed to the wealthiest elements of New York society and numbered among its officers Peter Cooper, Cornelius Vanderbilt, and August Belmont. The involvement of some of the wealthiest men in the country meant that the SPCC had strong financial backing and also made it clear that it was an essentially conservative undertaking. In 1882 Gerry explained to the National Conference of Charities and Corrections the purpose of cruelty societies and how and under what circumstances they functioned:

[Cruelty societies] are composed of humane persons of social position, unquestioned integrity and undoubted zeal. They interfere only when the law authorizes their interference for the benefit of the child; and they assert alike in their teaching and in their practice, the existence of the axiom that at the present day in this country, children have *some* rights, which even parents are bound to respect. . . . No matter how exalted the offender, the society has the right to confront him with its proofs; no matter how degraded the object of its mercy, the society is bound by its corporate duty to stretch out its hand and rescue from starvation, misery, cruelty, and perhaps death, the helpless little child who ought to have a protector, but for some reason, not its fault, has been deprived of that advantage.[20]

Early critics of the new organization feared that it would attack or undermine the family (despite the fact that the legal power to do so, *parens patriae,* had been long established). The founders tooks pains to assure New York City residents that they did not wish to interfere in traditional family life. They even felt it necessary to uphold the idea of corporal punishment as an acceptable part of family life. "A good wholesome flogging," Henry Bergh said, would be appropriate for "disobedient children."[21]

Like Charles Loring Brace of the CAS, the founders of the SPCC believed that they were not attacking the basis of family life or invading the sanctity of the family. They justified their actions as protecting the future of children in danger. While the founders endorsed appropriate corporal punishment, the SPCC was founded at a time when there was growing interest in eliminating corporal punishment and family violence in general.

Elizabeth Pleck likens the crusade against family violence to a similar movement in Massachusetts in the 1640s, but she attributes the later movement to "rising social dependency and disorder." She contends that "more favorable attitudes towards government intervention were coupled with a belief that the family was facing a major crisis." At any rate, the essentially conservative message of the SPCC inspired the founding of similar agencies in Boston and Philadelphia, and they in turn spawned others. By the end of the nineteenth century, SPCCs were common throughout the country.[22]

The SPCCs focused on physical abuse in their public campaigns because the public responded to that issue; but their definition of cruelty included a great many other activities. In 1884 the Brooklyn SPCC defined "cruelty" as:

a. all treatment or conduct by which physical pain is wrongfully, needlessly, or excessively inflicted, or

b. by which life or limb or health is wrongfully endangered or sacrificed, or

c.   neglect to provide such reasonable food, clothing, shelter, protection, and care as the life and well-being of the child require;

d.   the exposure of children during unreasonable hours of inclement weather, as peddlers or hawkers, or otherwise;

e.   their employment in unwholesome, degrading, or unlawful callings;

f.   or any employment by which the powers of children are over-taxed or their hours of labor unreasonably prolonged; and

g.   the employment of children as mendicants, or the failure to restrain them from vagrancy or begging.[23]

From this list we can see that the definition of cruelty implied a kind of bill of rights for children. They had the right to be free from excessive (presumably to be defined by the courts) physical abuse. They had a right to the basic necessities of life, and there is a recognition of a right to develop, which included the right to be free from harmful or dangerous employment.

How did it happen that these particular rights came to be advocated by an elitist philanthropic organization? In some respects the rights illuminated in this list were not new to the Anglo-American legal tradition. Certainly during the early part of the nineteenth century the power of *parens patriae* had come into play in the creation of the house of refuge; but refuges only received children, they did not intervene on behalf of children. CASs placed children out in rural locales, even sometimes taking children from intact families, and they tried to remove children from the streets. But they did not see themselves as child advocates. CASs saw themselves as saving children, but they defended their actions primarily as a way to reduce crime on the streets; their message implied that their main purpose was to ship "street Arabs" out west. As a secondary goal, they helped girls learn a respectable trade such as sewing. Only when the SPCC appeared did a clear-cut doctrine of child saving appear. The SPCC was the first to articulate the idea of enforcing children's rights against their parents. As Gerry said in 1882, "Children have *some* rights."

A look at the workings of the SPCC can help explain why the specific articulation of children's rights came so late in the nineteenth century. The SPCC copied the operating style of the SPCA, a quasi-police style that seemed to convey an impressive amount of power to its agents. Many of the agents were former policemen or firemen with no special training in child welfare work. Upon receipt of a complaint, an agent would investigate, frequently talking to neighbors and employers before going to the family in question. Agents might take no action, issue a warning, or remove the abused or neglected child.

So what did an SPCC typically do? When the agents decided the complaints had been brought out of spite or revenge, the society did nothing. The society also did nothing if the agent decided that the child deserved a beating or that the incident was insignificant. In general, the agents tended to side with the parents if the child was unruly, and with the husband if the wife had done anything that in the agent's mind justified a beating. Sometimes the society would remove children from their parents. According to Pleck, "Three out of every ten children's cases led to the placement of the child outside the home." Most of these children had been neglected and were subsequently placed in children's institutions.[24]

The placement of neglected or abused (or in some cases, abusive) children in children's institutions such as the New York House of Refuge did not advance the concept of children's rights, and some early child advocates criticized the societies for this action. A notable critic was the social work pioneer, Homer Folks, who found the use of institutions by the SPCCs understandable but "unfortunate." He concluded, however, that the societies' "greatest beneficence has been, not to the children who have come under their care, but to the vastly larger number whose parents have restrained angry tempers and vicious impulses through fear of 'the Cruelty.'"[25]

According to other students of the SPCC movement, the societies' development was "widely perceived as an attack on the family economy of the poor." The Philadelphia labor press regarded such agencies with cynicism, claiming that the Pennsylvania SPCC was "not much better than a fraud" because the well-to-do philanthropists who were busy saving children on the one hand ignored the evils of child labor in factories on the other. Working-class families had their own standards of respectability and put "the Cruelty" on a par with the police—to be called in only as a last resort. Working-class neighborhoods tended to be more close-knit than middle- and upper-class districts, and neighbors who became aware of abuse or neglect tried to remedy these cases before calling in outside help.[26] According to Linda Gordon, a historian who, like Elizabeth Pleck, has written about family violence, "Some cases of cruelty to children arose from disagreement about proper child raising," while others "arose from the inevitable cruelties of poverty." Such cruelties included "disease and malnutrition, children left unattended while their parents worked, children not warmly dressed, houses without heat, bedding crawling with vermin, unchanged diapers, injuries left without medical treatment."[27]

Thus, the SPCCs could also be seen as a middle- and upper-class effort to impose standards of respectability on poorer neighborhoods without understanding that poor people had and enforced their own codes of respectability and propriety. To be sure, there were poor people who seemed to lack any semblance of respectability and who were held in contempt by respectable members of the working class. It sometimes seemed, however, that this latter group was the only one the outside reformers perceived.[28]

To their lasting credit, SPCCs did raise the question of children's rights and did publicize the worst kinds of abuse. They began to address the question of neglect as well. In spite of their limitations, they deserve a place in the history of the advance of children's rights.

Conclusion

This chapter has traced the development of public schools, houses of refuge, CASs, and SPCCs. The rise of these institutions reflected profound changes in the way society related to families and their members. No longer was the family the primary institution of society responsible virtually alone for the health and welfare of its members and for society as a whole. Schools supplemented the educational function of the family and brought both a measure of social control over children and the opportunity for advancement. In the world of manifest destiny and rugged individualism, schools represented a social investment in the individual male child that would enable him to surpass his father. Girls went to school so that they could become better mothers. Education, its early advocates believed, would solve social problems and guarantee a bright future.

But schools did not succeed with certain children who needed more attention. These young offenders called attention to themselves by virtue of their behavior. The state, prompted by a coterie of prominent citizens, proposed to fix whatever was wrong with them and thereby "reform" their character. To do this, the state had to exercise the power of *parens patriae* and snatch children from the dangerous course they were on.

Getting a conviction in a court, easy as it was, did not address the problems of children who seemed to be living by their wits on city streets in the middle of the nineteenth century. CASs sprang up basically to rid the streets of these disturbing reminders that the expansion of the American economy and the American city had taken a terrible toll on the families of the lower orders.

The goal of clearing the streets, an impossible idea at best, left at issue the question of what should be done about children whose parents abused or neglected them in their own homes. To address this problem, SPCCs, motivated by a concern for children's welfare similar to the concern of animal protection societies, were established. The significant contribution of these societies was to put forward the claim of children for "*some* rights." The idea that children had rights of their own received formal public expression, though it must be added that in practice the rights of children seem not to have been the foremost concern of the societies.

The nineteenth century saw the growth and expansion of the concept of *parens patriae*—the legal underpinning of the state's authority to assert and enforce children's rights. It also saw the development of a greater social sensitivity to children and their needs. Some authorities have argued that this sensitivity arose from a greater romantic sensibility in society in general. In any case, the century ended with a renewed commitment to the welfare of children as some reformers proclaimed the twentieth century would be "the century of the child."

Chapter Three

The Age of the Child, 1890–1920

The Progressive Era—the last decade of the nineteenth century and the first two decades of the twentieth century in the United States—was a great watershed so far as social policy toward children and children's rights were concerned. It was an age of reform and of clear concern about what was happening to American society, to American values, and especially to American children. It was also an age of optimism. Reformers and experts (sometimes they were one and the same) believed that a new and better age was about to dawn and that they had the means to shape it through their ideas and actions. Professionals believed that they had the necessary expertise to recast society along efficient, orderly, and effective lines. Reformers, muckrakers, ambitious politicians, earnest social workers (usually well-educated single women), and even club women from the upper classes all supported the exposure of graft and corruption in the political system and reform efforts to clean up the mess.

Powerful class and ethnic issues were also raised during the Progressive Era. Most of the reformers and experts came from the middle classes, and most were native-born white Protestants. Most of the targets of the reform efforts were either immigrant families and children or political bosses whose power depended on organizing the votes of immigrants. To working-class and immigrant families, the social workers, journalists, and club women—progressives all—seemed to be cut from the same cloth as the founders and agents of the SPCCs. These earnest social improvers seemed to want the working and immigrant classes to adopt middle-class ways. Despite these class-bound tendencies, reformers created new institutions, such as the juvenile court, attacked genuine social evils, such as child labor, and broadened the base of social action on behalf of the less fortunate by such efforts as extending the school year and making school attendance compulsory.

The Rise of Child Experts

Prior to the late nineteenth century, experts on children were typically ministers whose advice reflected dominant attitudes about child rearing and, by extension, social attitudes about children. By the end of the century, however, "professional" experts such as psychologists and social workers had appeared. They and a host of well-meaning volunteers combined forces and became "child savers," as one study has labeled them.[1]

The previous generation of child workers might well have been called the "institution builders." Their conception of children derived from the influence of the Enlightenment thinking, which emphasized reason and viewed children as morally neutral and thus capable of moral improvement through institutional incarceration and discipline. The child savers, by contrast, held a romantic view of children as "beings from God" who, if anything, were morally superior to adults and who represented the future of American society. They sought to remove children from evil contexts, hoping in the process to create a sounder, better society that would be safe for children. The child savers came mostly from the middle classes and, like the institution builders, focused on the problems of working-class and immigrant families.

Viviana Zelizer has described the process whereby children were transformed from economic assets for working-class families into "sacralized" beings whose value transcended the marketplace. "The social construction of the economically useless child" was achieved through legislation, vigorous enforcement of new laws, the creation of the juvenile court, and a profound change in cultural attitudes about children. As children became economically useless, their emotional and psychological value increased.[2] From a sensitive reading of children's literature, historian Bernard Wishy reaches a similar conclusion; he argues that from about 1870 on, "the sentimental notion that somehow it is better to be a child than an adult, that the best standards of life are those of naive and innocent children becomes an increasingly powerful theme in American culture."[3]

One of the most important texts of the era was *Children's Rights* (1892) by Kate Douglas Wiggin (who is best known for her *Rebecca of*

Sunnybrook Farm). Wiggin precisely documented the sentimentalization of childhood and urged a realistic view of children, though she cautioned against excessive moralism: "As to keeping children too clean for any mortal use, I suppose nothing is more disastrous. The divine right to be gloriously dirty a large portion of the time, when dirt is a necessary consequence of direct, useful, friendly contact with all sorts of interesting, helpful things, is too clear to be denied." Wiggin also urged a gentler approach to discipline, claiming that "it seems likely that the rod of reason will have to replace the rod of birch."[4]

Children became more sentimentalized (and sacralized) at the end of the nineteenth century because people believed that by saving the children they could improve the future. Almost literally, then, children were society's best hope. If the romantic view of children as both morally superior to adults and capable of instructing adults was to have a significant social impact, it would be in the form of a great amount of attention being paid to the lives of actual children. While romanticism might have stimulated this kind of attention, it remained to be seen whether or not the well-meaning progressives would in fact accept instruction from the tiny citizens of American society.

The Professionalization of Psychology and Social Work

One of the major characteristics of the Progressive Era was the restructuring—the professionalization—of the production of knowledge in both applied and academic endeavors. The principal talisman of this process was the creation of professional associations, as the following list of founding dates illustrates:

1876	American Chemical Society
1880	American Society of Chemical Engineers
1882	American Forestry Association
1883	American Ornithologists' Union
1884	American Climatological Society
1885	American Institute of Electrical Engineers
1888	Geological Society of America
1888	National Statistical Association
1888	American Mathematical Society
1889	American Physical Society[5]

According to Burton Bledstein, professionals sought a kind of "autonomous individualism, a position of unchallenged authority." A profession, Bledstein explains, was "a full-time occupation" from which one earned a substantial income and enjoyed a large measure of autonomy. This autonomy came as a result of the professional's having "mastered an esoteric but useful body of systematic knowledge, completed theoretical training before entering a practice or apprenticeship, and received a degree or license from a recognized institution." These accomplishments allowed professionals to claim special social privileges and powers, but "professionalism also implied an ethic of service which meant that the interest of the client was supposed to take precedence over the ideal of personal profit."[6]

The process of professionalization can be seen clearly in the rise of interest in children as objects of study. A fairly informal movement to study children, using mothers as observers, began under the supervision of G. Stanley Hall, the president of Clark University and one of the country's first professional psychologists. In 1883 Hall published *The Contents of Children's Minds,* a study of what children know before entering school. The study was based on a list of 123 questions asked of kindergarten children in Boston and became so popular that Hall decided to launch a movement in order to gather the data necessary to construct a scientific (and professional) view of the child.

The child study movement began in the 1880s and reached its zenith in the 1890s as Hall toured the country giving lectures to mothers and teachers. His method was to develop a series of questions on such topics as playing with dolls, children's lies, and children's fears. Correspondents around the country would fill out the forms and return them for Hall and his students to analyze. Hall believed that the material thus gathered would clearly illustrate his pet theory that children relive the stages of human history. The child study movement faded, however, before Hall could confirm his theory. The movement was significant, however, because of its focus on children. Studying children came from a romantic impulse; but like many other good intentions, the original purpose (to take children seriously) got lost—in this case, in the effort to create professional knowledge.

Hall abandoned the child study movement in part because it was based on the observations of amateurs. But the increased interest in children and in the moral character of society as a whole lived on. There were others also looking for scientific knowledge about children, notably, John Frederick Herbart, a German educator who emphasized the need for the study of child psychology as a preparation for instruction. Herbart was a transitional figure in the history of psychology, which he saw as an empirical science but not an experimental one.

The honor of being the first "scientific" psychologist belongs to Wilhelm Wundt, who founded the first formal psychological laboratory in Leipzig in 1879. According to Edward G. Boring, Wundt's laboratory was the fountainhead of most early psychological training. Studying there were "not only Germans like Kraepelin, Lehman, Kelpe and Meumann, but also the majority of the first generation of experimentalists in America, men like Stanley Hall, Cattell, Scripture, Frank Angell, Titchener, Witmer, Warren, Stratton, and Judd." The Americans who studied with Wundt brought the experimental tradition back to the United States and thus helped to establish the profession of psychology.[7]

The appearance of professional psychology in the United States gave added impetus to the scientific study of the child. Most notable among the psychologists pursuing such study (besides Hall, who was preeminent) was James Mark Baldwin of Princeton. Baldwin argued, like Hall, that "genetic [developmental] psychology ought to lay the only solid foundation for education."[8] Baldwin, Hall, and Herbart propounded this idea, but John Dewey would be the first to actually apply psychological theory to the practice of education.

Dewey was a central figure in the laboratory school at the University of Chicago. In one of his most famous works, *School and Society* (1899), he argued that the school was, in effect, "an embryonic society." The essential process of education was "to lay hold upon the rudimentary instincts of human nature, and, by supplying a proper medium, so control their expressions as . . . to facilitate and enrich the growth of the individual child." Dewey wanted to "psychologize" the schools and bring children under the care of professional teachers because "the occupations and relationships of the home environment are not specially selected for the growth of the child."[9]

"We have first to fix attention upon the child," Dewey wrote in 1897, "to find out what kind of experience is appropriate to him at the particular period selected." The procedure Dewey recommended was direct observation. "We endeavor by observation and reflection to see what tastes and powers of the child are active. . . . We ask what habits are being formed; what ends and aims are being proposed." In short, Dewey proposed to begin the process of studying educational reform by studying children.[10]

Dewey moved to Teachers' College of Columbia University in 1904 and there joined a faculty among whom the idea of using psychology as a way of developing scientific knowledge about children had been promoted by Edward L. Thorndike. Thorndike was a strong proponent of measurement as the basis for knowledge. He believed that the function of the schools was to identify the talented students, and that the role of psychology was to supply the means for that identification. Thorndike took strong exception to Dewey's central ideas. In *Educational Psychology* (1913) he wrote, "The one thing that educational theorists of today seem to place as the foremost duty of the schools—the development of powers and capacities—is the one thing that schools or any other educational forces can do least." Schools "help society in general tremendously," he wrote, "by providing it not with better men, but with the knowledge of which men are good."[11]

While the professionalization of psychology added another important element to the mix of concerns about children in the Progressive Era, there were a number of new professionals like Thorndike who believed that child study would serve primarily as a means of sorting children into categories. For Thorndike and many like him, the school was a means of classifying students rather than an instrument for the reform of society. "I am sure that we could pick out mentally gifted men or children," he wrote, "more successfully by ten minutes observation of their facial expression, manners and opinions than by a day's work in measuring any combination of anatomical traits or motor activities." Quite clearly, the reform sentiments of those like Dewey included a recognition of children's rights, and the ideas of the more conservative test-and-measure branch of educational psychology did not.[12]

In the Progressive Era psychology was emerging as an academic specialty. Meanwhile, various volunteers in charity and philanthropic work sought to professionalize their work. They had already begun to label their activities "scientific philanthropy." In 1892 Zilpha Smith of the Boston Associated Charities organized classes for social workers, explaining that the work had become so complicated that it required training. Several other social workers advanced the cause by advocating training, and by 1903 the University of Chicago had created the Institute of Social Science for that purpose. A second strand of social work, the development of the settlement house, represented the practical, hands-on approach to the professionalization of social knowledge. From this tradition no less an authority than Jane Addams argued that child labor, for instance, was a problem that required professional analysis.

These two strands came together around the turn of the century when, in 1897, Mary Richmond, the future author of the path-breaking text *Social Diagnosis,* told the National Conference of Charities and Corrections that social workers needed a professional education comparable to that given to medical students. The creation of a special summer course in New York sponsored by that city's Charity Organization Society and the founding of the New York School of Philanthropy in 1904 completed the process.[13]

The professionalization of psychology and social work in this period marked the beginnings of specialization in the production of knowledge. As knowledge became more fragmented, and as the variety of perspectives on the child increased, it seemed as if the object of all this activity became fragmented, too. As a consequence of professionalization, the romantic view of the child lost ground to an emerging "scientific" view. Children who had formerly been on the pedestal of moral superiority now found themselves beneath the microscope of professional scrutiny. If Kate Douglas Wiggin wished to indulge children in their love of dirt, John Dewey and Jane Addams wished to alter the child's environment at school and in society and by doing so, transform the world. In Wiggin's view, children had the right to be themselves. Dewey's children would be observed and then improved. The question of rights did not appear to be an issue for the new professionals.

Institutional Reform: The Creation of the Juvenile Court

Most social workers, whether volunteers or newly trained professionals, saw their work as essentially practical. They might have been thoroughly familiar with the application of Darwin's theory of evolution to society, but their actions indicated a strong willingness to work for amelioration in the present rather than wait for the inexorable laws of nature to take their course.

When social workers and club women in Chicago focused on the circumstances under which children came to the notice of the police, they were appalled. They could hardly ignore the appearance of a sensational work, *If Christ Came to Chicago* (1894), by British journalist William T. Stead. "There is very little reverence for children in Chicago," Stead wrote, citing cases of youthful boys carrying messages in and out of the jail or selling newspapers in the city's bordellos.[14] The combined efforts of such organizations as the Chicago Visitation and Aid Society, the Waif's Mission, and the Chicago Women's Club led to the creation of a separate school for boys in the Cook County House of Correction. While this school was an improvement for those detained, the Women's Club, inspired by the development of probation for juvenile offenders in Massachusetts, worked for the creation of a separate trial court for juvenile offenders in Chicago. The act creating the court, the first of its kind in the United States, passed the Illinois legislature in July 1899.[15]

In the arena of children's rights, the Illinois Juvenile Court Act of 1899 was a major milestone. According to the law, a delinquent child was a child under 16 who had violated the law or a city or village ordinance. The act created a special court in Chicago and guaranteed the right to a trial by jury, although this latter right had to be requested. The law also provided that "any respectable person" who knew of a child who "appears to be either neglected, dependent, or delinquent" could complain to the court. The court had broad powers and could remove children from their homes and place them in institutions, with charitable agencies, in foster homes, or on probation. The most important part of the law was the last section: "This act shall be liberally construed to the end that its purpose may be carried out, to wit: That the care, custody and discipline of a child shall approximate as nearly as may be that which should be given by its parents, and in all cases where it can properly be done the child placed in an improved family home and become a member of the family by legal adoption or otherwise."[16] Not only were the powers of the court broad, the intent of the legislation was to create a flexible, active institution that would function (so it was hoped) in the best interests of the child.

Soon after the court began operating, the backers of the court and the first judge, Richard S. Tuthill, realized that the definition of delinquency was too restrictive and would require the court to function more like a criminal court. An amendment revising the definition of delinquency was added to the basic law in 1901 and stipulated that a delinquent was a child under the age of 16 who breaks the law or "who is incorrigible; or who knowingly associates with thieves, vicious or immoral persons; or who is growing up in idleness or crime; or who frequents a house of ill-fame; or who knowingly patronizes any policy shop or place where any gaming device is, or shall be operated."[17]

The creation of the juvenile court was one of the crowning achievements of progressive reform in the United States. Progressive reformers, well-meaning club women, and members of the local political establishment had combined forces to develop an institution that would put the interests and needs of the child first. This rosy view of the juvenile court stemmed from the enthusiasm of its early supporters. Critics appeared, however, soon after the court began. The first challenge to the legality of the juvenile court came in Pennsylvania in the case of *Commonwealth* v. *Fisher* in 1906, in which the Pennsylvania Supreme Court found the juvenile court to be an acceptable implementation of the principle of *parens patriae*. Others objected to the broad powers given the court, charging it with getting too far away from the criminal law.[18]

The critics had a point. The court may have been created to protect children from abuse and to save children whose actions seemed to put them at risk, but it acted in the best interests of the child without necessarily taking the child's rights or the rights of parents into consideration. Consider, for example, a Mrs. Wilowski's case, which was heard in Milwaukee in 1916. She was brought into court on a charge of neglect. Her husband was suffering from tuberculosis, and she had been having difficulty with health officials who wanted to examine her children. She preferred her own doctor. The judge ordered the children brought into court. The mother refused. "I ain't no sinner," she said, "no drinker; I support my children so long, and I want to stay with them." Eventually she gave in to the judge, and she and her children were placed under the supervision of a probation officer.[19]

Sometimes parents who could afford it brought in lawyers who asserted the rights of their clients, with some limited effect. According to Steven Schlossman, "Attorneys could help, but only up to a point." The power of the judge in a juvenile court was for all practical purposes unlimited. The ineffectiveness of lawyers was but one piece of evidence that juvenile courts rarely considered children's rights. There were all sorts of abuses in juvenile courts, including improper questions and widespread use of "hearsay and circumstantial evidence." The officers of the court "placed children in double jeopardy, 'convicted' them of prior offenses, and used confessions to further implicate them and their parents." Defenders of the court claimed that it needed all this information to develop a "sophisticated diagnosis" of a child's needs. The net "effect of these inquiries was to incriminate defendants and their parents in innumerable misdeeds—moral, criminal, or otherwise—for which they could be held liable." Schlossman concludes that "instead of eliminating all trappings of criminal procedure, especially the concern with guilt or innocence, the juvenile court eliminated mainly those due process safeguards with which children and parents could defend themselves."[20]

The creation of the juvenile court and the professionalization of psychology and social work marked the midpoint of progressive efforts to develop the expertise and means to reshape society along more morally acceptable lines. One of the central concerns of progressivism was the child. In particular, the social wing of progressivism sought to improve the lives of children and by that device improve the future. A second group of progressives sought improvement by reforming the structure of society. The creation of the juvenile court was an example of the intersection of these two kinds of reform during the Progressive Era.

The conflict between the child savers' romantic belief in children's innate goodness and the institution builders' Lockean notion of children as neutral beings open to moral improvement, given the right environment, was resolved by many progressive reformers by the adoption of a new belief: that most children (especially immigrant and black children) are innately depraved. Buttressed by the views of Sigmund Freud, who believed children are "polymorphously perverse," these reformers thought the task of society was to identify those children who could be counted on to become the leaders of the future. They in turn would learn, according to Thorndike, "obedience to the right masters, imitation of the right models, and learning of the right facts in our schools." Professional psychologists and social workers stood ready to be masters, models, and purveyors of the right facts.[21]

The Battle of the Sandbox: The Fight over Kindergartens

Nowhere was the fight over the inner nature of the child more intense than in the struggle over the purpose and curriculum of the "child's garden." Begun in a romantic tradition, the kindergarten owed much of its early history and development to the ideas and efforts of the German educator Friedrich Froebel.

The kindergarten was introduced to the United States in 1855 and became very popular in the late nineteenth century. The leading advocates of the kindergarten were romantic idealists associated with the transcendentalist movement around Boston and included Elizabeth Peabody, Mary Peabody Mann, Bronson Alcott, and Susan Blow. According to Dominick Cavallo, a historian of the kindergarten movement, "More than anything else these pioneers of the American kindergarten held in common an unshakable belief in the child's potential for spiritual—or moral perfection."[22]

These early "kindergartners" (advocates of the new institution) strongly supported the family as a means of protecting the child from the harshness of modern materialism. They idealized the mother's role and believed that the kindergarten teacher would replicate the role of mother in the ideal family. The kindergarten would supplement the home and do what a busy mother who probably had other children to care for could not do herself.

At first kindergartens were private operations that appealed to the upper classes. By the 1870s, however, kindergartners developed charity kindergartens designed to save the children of inadequate mothers. If mothers were "too busy, too ignorant, too poor, or too foreign," kindergartners stood ready to step in and expose working-class children to the benefits of middle-class attitudes and practices. The kindergartners also sought to develop a strong personal sense of morality in their charges, while emphasizing their connectedness to society as a whole.

The focus on the individual development of the child marked the early kindergartners as romantic in their orientation. With the growth of professionalization in the late nineteenth century, the idealized view of the purpose of the kindergarten did not go long unchallenged. The opening salvo in the "battle of the sandbox" was fired by progressive reformers who challenged the idea that the home is the proper place to rear children.

Imbued with the spirit of science and claiming a license to intervene in society to create a better future, a new generation of kindergartners challenged the old romantic notions of the founders. "To progressives," Cavallo has written, "the individual's intellect and emotions were not only measureable, but the quests for both social order and unity made calculations of human desires, drives, abilities, and potential behaviors necessary."[23] These kindergartners found the theories and ideas of Thorndike and Dewey ready-made for their purposes. To build a better society they were willing to cast out a child-centered curriculum based on the innate goodness of the child. These progressives were far less concerned with children's rights than with taking action for societal improvement.

In this context, Kate Douglas Wiggin published *Children's Rights,* a defense of the older, romantic view of the nature and purpose of the kindergarten. She wanted a child-centered kindergarten, but she agreed with both the romantic and the scientific reformers that one of the primary functions of the kindergarten should be "to help in the absorption and amalgamation of our foreign element." She believed that kindergarten would correct the "moral blight" of "an unfortunate little waif," and concluded that "the child of poverty and vice has still within him, however overlaid by the sins of ancestry, a germ of good that is capable of growth, if reached in time."[24]

So, in effect, the battle of the sandbox was a battle of priorities: Would kindergarten policy, and by extension other social policies, derive from the future needs of society, as articulated by the professionals, or would policy be essentially child-centered? Would the Progressive Era's focus be on children's rights or on society's future needs? The answer proved to be complicated. Even as the romantics lost the fight over the kindergarten, other reformers, motivated by a genuine concern for the health and safety of children, mounted campaigns to improve health and eliminate the evil of child labor.

Conclusion

The development of "scientific" knowledge about children during the Progressive Era served two separate functions. On the one hand, it led to the rise of new academic disciplines devoted to increasing knowledge about children and about human growth and development. On the other hand, this new knowledge seemed to give reformers the means they needed to transform society. To know the child was to understand the instrument that society would use to create a better future.

The father of the scientific study of the child was G. Stanley Hall, author of the first text on adolescence and the distinguished president of Clark University. Even more significant than Hall, however, were John Dewey, with his emphasis on progressive education, and Edward L. Thorndike, who stressed the importance of measurement and classification in the schools.

Following in the footsteps of psychologists, social workers also sought to develop professional status. Just as psychologists were experts on human behavior and human development, so would social workers become experts on human society. In combination, these professionals would develop the knowledge necessary to rid society of the evils spawned by the rigid industrialization of the United States in the late nineteenth century.

To fix social ills, reformers would begin with children. If you agreed with Dewey, the schools had to be transformed; if you agreed with Thorndike, they had to become better at sorting out the winners. Also, families had to be instructed in the proper care and nurture of children. The institution created to accomplish this was the juvenile court. It regulated the lives of those children who came to its attention, with no regard for formal notions of rights or due process.

To some reformers, the creation of the juvenile court and the development of new expertise in child psychology and social work meant that the aims and purposes of society were taking precedence over the needs, interests, and rights of children. The new knowledge and the new institutions did work "in the best interest of the child," but the definition of that interest now belonged to the experts. Romantics such as Kate

Douglas Wiggin urged a fuzzier, more sentimental view of children, but the experts, fired by the growth in knowledge and expertise, proceeded to regulate and codify children's lives in a host of ways.

As a result of the juvenile court, children probably lost some legal guarantees on such issues as formal due process and the like. At the same time, they gained an institution that could represent their interests even against their own parents. The creation of the juvenile court did not mean the elimination of such basic rights as life, the right to be free from abuse, or the right to a decent start in life.

Chapter Four

Children and the Federal Government: The Campaign against Child Labor, 1900–1938

Unlike previous chapters, this one departs from the chronological march to focus on a single subject through several periods. While the campaign to eliminate child labor was waged during the first half of the twentieth century (and has continued sporadically down to the present), it is a subject that requires a separate discussion. This chapter focuses not only on child labor but on the effort to achieve federal regulation of it.

Of all the progressive crusades, none captured the public imagination more than the effort to eliminate child labor. Thanks in part to the graphic and effecting photographs of Jacob Riis and Lewis Hine, the public came to see and understand the impact of industrial society on American children. As a result, the aroused public and the coalition of experts and reformers reached a powerful consensus that child labor was an intrinsically evil activity, and that the forces of society should be mobilized against it.

Although the reformers and crusaders did not define a right for children to be free from harmful or dangerous labor before a certain age, the effect of their efforts was to achieve this right. By the end of the nineteenth century, children had the right to life, the right to be free from abuse, and a claim if not a right to middle-class status. Parents demonstrated that their children did not work by dressing them in fancy, frilly clothing. Middle-class children also attended school more frequently and longer than did working-class children. Throughout most of the nine-teenth century, however, most middle-class families did not pay a great deal of attention to working children of the working classes, although members of the middle class lent their support to the public school move-ment and other reform efforts aimed at eliminating crime and poverty by improving the lives of working-class children. Even when Charles Loring Brace and other midcentury reformers began to provide services and placement in foster families for urban children, they did not raise the issue of child labor. Indeed, Brace, far from opposing child labor, en-couraged it through the policies of his Newsboys Lodging House, which charged for its services (and lent money at interest to boys who were temporarily short of cash).[1]

Only after working-class and immigrant families came under the scru-tiny of social workers and experts was the issue of child labor taken seriously. After American society had sacralized children, middle-class Americans came to believe that labor by children from intact families was also a social evil. Brace and his ilk had sought to deal with orphaned children who lived by their wits on city streets; now society would ad-dress the issue of children from intact families working in factories or in other dangerous activities. To see child labor as a problem required a new way of thinking. The basic attitude toward poverty and social misery was that people had brought their misery on themselves through idle-ness, laziness, or character defects. The cure for poverty, in this view, was hard work and thrift.[2]

In 1899 Jane Addams argued for an altered view of child labor. "It has long been a common error for the charity visitor," she wrote, "to sug-gest, or at least connive, that the children be put to work early. . . ." She continued: "It is so easy, after one has been taking the industrial view for a long time, to forget the larger and more social claim; to urge that the boy go to work and support his parents who are receiving char-itable aid." The problem was that the visitor did not "realize what a cruel advantage the person who distributes charity has, when she gives ad-vice." Thus, the charity visitor was "eager to seize any crutch, however weak, which might enable them to get on. She failed to see that the boy who attempts prematurely to support his widowed mother may lower wages, add an illiterate member to the community, and arrest the de-velopment of a capable workman."[3]

From the beginning of American society, most children have started to work as soon as they were able. Work inside a household generally did not bring any comment from the larger community unless there were some clear indications of abuse. Hard, even dangerous work did not by itself constitute abuse as defined in preindustrial America. The coming of the factory system, however, created new conditions for children's work. Americans learned from the English experience; child labor was a central part of the expansion of British industry, and gradually English reformers came to see the exploitation of children as a great social evil. After long experience with the abuses and dangers of the practice of employing children in factories, late nineteenth–century American reformers came around to the same point of view.

Children were among the first factory workers in the United States. According to historian Walter Trattner, factory owners preferred to hire children because they were cheap labor and because they were thought to be "more tractable, reliable and industrious, quicker, neater, and more careful, and as labor unions developed, less likely to strike."[4] The first reaction to the practice of employing children in factories (and the one that proved to be the most effective means of dealing with child labor) was to draw up laws requiring a certain amount of schooling for children. Connecticut passed a law in 1813 requiring basic instruction for children in factories. Massachusetts passed a similar law in the 1830s, and by 1850 so had Rhode Island and Pennsylvania.[5]

By the middle of the nineteenth century, a web of legislation regulating child labor had been passed in northern states. According to Trattner, "Many of the fundamentals of child labor reform were already present" by that time, including acceptance of the idea that a child had a "right to secure an education and be protected from exploitation." Nevertheless, Trattner continues, "early government measures did little to translate rights into realities. To begin with, they required no proof of age. Most contained no enforcement provisions, and their wording was so ambiguous that employees could easily circumvent them."[6] There were also many loopholes. Parental consent could negate the effect of the laws, which in any event did not apply to orphans. The loopholes and the lack of effective enforcement reflected the gap between public intentions as reflected in the legislation and the prevailing attitude toward child labor. Probably most Americans thought that children should learn good work habits as early as practicable. In addition, there continued to be a great reluctance to interfere in families, even in cases of child abuse.

Many families would have preferred to keep their children out of the work force so that they could attain the education and advantages they would need to move up the social ladder. The overwhelming popularity of education among the working classes is a powerful testament to their desire to improve the lot of their children. At the same time, however, low wages and the seasonal nature of factory work forced families to grasp every available means of bringing in income, including relying on the labor of their children.

The tremendous expansion of the manufacturing sector of the American economy in the last half of the nineteenth century, accompanied by an equally rapid growth in immigration, led to a comparable expansion of the work force. Children filled many of the new places in the factories and everywhere else small hands and quick feet could be put to use.

In the 1870s reformers began to address the problems of child labor. Charles Loring Brace described the ways in which the child labor laws were evaded, even though he believed that lower-class children should support themselves. Labor unions, including the Knights of Labor and the Workingmen's Assembly in New York City, took up the issue of child labor. The new concern prompted New York to pass a compulsory school attendance law in 1874; the act required 14 weeks of school attendance per year but lacked provisions for proof of age and adequate enforcement.

In 1882 Elbridge Gerry of the SPCC and Dr. Abraham Jacobi, president of the New York State Medical Association, sponsored a bill to prevent children under 14 from working at all. It also required a medical examination and forbade the employment of children in dangerous industries such as glassworks or brickyards. The bill was killed in the state legislature. According to Jeremy Felt, the bill and other related legislation failed to pass because reformers were "unable to mobilize public opinion against child labor." Ordinary citizens were unaware of the extent of child labor and most "believed that a comparatively small number of children were working to support needy parents."[7]

The effort to arouse public opinion and win legislative fights over child labor took a different direction in New York in the 1880s after efforts to regulate the production of cigars in tenements (a practice that involved many children and was very harmful to their health) failed twice. The creation of a state bureau of labor statistics in 1883 was also significant because it began to provide the data reformers would use to heighten public awareness of the extent of child labor.

The reformers kept trying. New York passed the Factory Act of 1886, which prohibited factory work by children under 13. The act also stipulated that children had to produce an affidavit attesting to their age. To enforce the act, two factory inspectors were appointed. Clearly two men could not effectively oversee the work force in the state's more than

42,000 factories. Not until well into the twentieth century did New York have an effective factory inspection system.

In Illinois, by contrast, Gov. John Peter Altgeld appointed the redoubtable Florence Kelley as the state's first chief factory inspector. Kelley, who had attended Cornell and the University of Zurich and was a prominent American socialist, quickly attracted attention when she became an agent for the state's bureau of labor statistics and began investigating the sweating system of clothing manufacture. In a letter to Friedrich Engels in 1892 she observed that the "work consists in shop visitation, followed by house to house visitation," and concluded that, "in the ward in which I live, the Nineteenth, with 7,000 children of school age (6–14 inclusive), there are but 2,579 school sittings and everything municipal is of the same sort. This aggravates the economic conditions greatly, making possible child labor in most cruel forms and rendering the tenement house manufacture of clothing a deadly danger to the whole community."[8]

Kelley, who had been described as a "smoking volcano," had by the time of her appointment as a special agent transformed Hull House, the Chicago settlement house made famous by Jane Addams, into a platform for social action. Another observer said of her: "No other man or woman whom I have ever heard so blended knowledge of facts, wit, satire, burning indignation, prophetic denunciation—all poured out at white heat in a voice varying from flute like tones to deep organ tones."[9]

Following Altgeld's defeat in the 1896 gubernatorial election, Kelley lost her job as factory inspector and was replaced by Louis Arrington of the notorious Illinois Glass Company, a firm well known for its widespread use of children in extremely dangerous jobs. Kelley turned her efforts to the Illinois Consumers' League and through it to the creation of a national consumer organization that would use the power of purchasing to exert influence on manufacturers. The hope was that such an organization might wield this power to eliminate child labor. The new organization, the National Federation of Consumers' Leagues, took shape in January 1899 in New York City, with Kelley as corresponding secretary. In effect, she was the primary staff person for the Consumers' League, and she used this position as a platform for her ideas. In 1902 she suggested that settlement workers in New York create a committee to tackle the problem of child labor. The committee included Kelley, Lillian Wald of the Henry Street Settlement, Mary K. Simkhovitch, Pauline Goldmark, and Robert Hunter of University Settlement.

This informal committee launched a small-scale investigation of child labor in the city of New York. The results led to the creation of the New

York Child Labor Committee, a permanent statewide organization with solid funding and backing from socially prominent citizens. The committee lost no time in sending a memorial to the legislature calling for a better factory law. Not content to rest its case on a single memorandum, the committee took its case to the public as well. It hired a press agent who issued a flood of case histories emphasizing the evils of child labor. Factory visits from committee members ensured that these new case histories would be followed with editorial emphasis. The committee peppered legislators with material about child labor and with letters supporting proposed legislation. The committee was very successful in this effort. In all, four bills that revised earlier laws passed the New York legislature in 1903. Although these bills attempted to close loopholes in the earlier laws, the problem of enforcement remained.

In one effort the committee had only limited success. A bill to regulate child labor in the street trades passed only after being much diluted. One reason a tougher version failed was that the child labor reformers came into conflict with Elbridge Gerry and the Society for the Prevention of Cruelty to Children. The SPCC regarded street children as their exclusive concern. In a hearing before the New York State Senate, Gerry pointed out that street trading was already against the law and added that his society would "take care" of any violators turned over to the police. In addition, judges from the children's court also complained about the difficulties of trying cases under the proposed law. Nevertheless, it was the first such bill passed in the country. [10]

Meanwhile, efforts to create a national committee similar to the one in New York State were under way. Felix Adler, founder of the ethical culture movement and a charter member of the New York child labor committee, became acquainted with Edgar Murphy of the Southern Education Board (which had offices in New York City). Murphy, an Episcopal clergyman, had led the effort to pass a new child labor law in Alabama in 1903. When he became secretary to the Southern Education Board and moved to New York, he found himself in contact with the right people to create a national organization. Murphy, Adler, William Baldwin, who was the president of the Long Island Railroad, and Florence Kelley became the provisional committee for a national organization. Their efforts quickly led to the creation of the National Child Labor Committee, which met for the first time on 15 April 1904.

Adler presided at that first meeting and argued that since child labor was a national problem, a national effort to defeat it was needed. He also indicated that the committee held the view that children had the right to be free from labor until age 12: "It should be plainly said that whatever happens in the sacrifice of adult workers, the public conscience inexorably demands that the children under twelve years of age shall not be touched; that childhood shall be sacred; that industrialism and commercialism shall not be allowed beyond this point to degrade humanity. Thus the function of the Committee will be a preventive one. By no other means than those that have been suggested can be needless sacrifice of child life be prevented."[11] Thus, the National Child Labor Committee viewed childhood as sacred. It would become one of the first national children's rights organizations. Unlike other such organizations, it would achieve its goal of effective federal legislation against child labor. In many respects, the National Child Labor Committee can be regarded as the prototype of protective child advocacy organizations.

The committee was national in scope, but the executive committee consisted of people in and around New York City: Adler, Baldwin, Kelley, and Murphy were all on the executive committee, along with a corporation lawyer, the president of a candy company, an investment banker, Edward T. Devine, general secretary of the New York Charity Organization Society, and John W. Wood, secretary of the Missionary Society of the Protestant Episcopal Church. The National Child Labor Committee was clearly in the vanguard of a national movement on behalf of children.[12] As the leading authority on the history of child labor reform indicated, "Committee members firmly believed that all people had a right to maximum physical, mental, and cultural development, [and] that society was responsible for the welfare of individuals."[13]

The committee began its work by gathering more information. Committee members did some preliminary scouting and concluded that the worst instances of child labor were to be found in the coal mines of Pennsylvania, in glass factories, and in southern cotton mills. They decided to concentrate on coal mining first. Pennsylvania had weak laws regulating child labor and a large concentration of school-age children. Further studies of the mines found a number of young teenagers employed legally in the mine and 10,000 younger children employed illegally in the mines and in the breakers. The work in the breakers was especially dangerous:

The boys sat for ten or eleven hours a day in rows on wooden boards placed over chutes through which tons of coal constantly passed. Their task was to pick out from the passing coal the slate, stone, and other waste that came from the mine. The slate so closely resembled the coal that it could be detected only by close scrutiny. The boys had to bend over the chute and reach down into it. Even if they wore gloves, which was not always possible because they frequently had to rely on a sense of touch, the moving material was so sharp that it could cut and tear their hands. The position in which the boys sat was not only tiring but backbreaking, causing obviously round shoulders and narrow chests. If a boy reached too far and slipped into the coal that flowed beneath him, he stood little chance of surviving intact.[14]

The committee began a campaign of education and publicized its findings, which eventually led to tougher legislation. The first new law, passed in 1905, required documentary proof of age for working children and some education, but it did not survive a court challenge. A successful law regulating child labor in anthracite coal mines was passed in Pennsylvania in 1909.[15]

Meanwhile, the New York committee also fought successfully to have a new state commissioner of labor named and developed a scholarship or compensation program whereby families would receive $1–3 a week to replace the earnings lost because children were no longer working. To receive the money, children had to provide documentary proof that they were in school.[16]

After a campaign against glass factory night work (which began to disappear as the glass industry modernized), the National Child Labor Committee turned its attention to southern cotton mills. Southern states had extremely permissive laws regulating child labor (Georgia, in fact, had no law at all). Conditions in the mills shocked an English reformer, Irene Ashby, who visited Alabama in the winter of 1900–1901. "I was prepared to find child labor," she wrote, "but one could hardly be prepared to find in America today white children six and seven years of age, working for twelve hours a day—aroused before daybreak and toiling, till long after sundown in winter, with only half an hour for rest and refreshment."[17]

The National Child Labor Committee began its investigations in 1905 and with the help of Alexander McKelway, the committee's secretary, drafted a bill to raise the minimum working age in factories to 14 for girls and illiterates and to prohibit night work for children under 14. The opposition of North Carolina mill owners killed the bill in congressional committee. The national committee gained a small victory in Georgia when that state finally passed a law in 1906 prohibiting factory work for children under 12 unless they had dependent parents. In no case was it legal for children under 10 to work.[18]

Meanwhile, Sen. Albert J. Beveridge of Indiana introduced a federal child labor bill in 1906. The national committee voted to support the Beveridge bill, although it was not ready to abandon efforts to secure legislation at the state level. Committee members sought to rally support behind the bill but learned that neither Samuel Gompers of the American Federation of Labor (AFL) nor Theodore Roosevelt supported it. Even the child labor reformers were divided over it. Roosevelt did support a federally funded study of the problem of child labor and a model bill for the District of Columbia. Beveridge pressed on with his bill, but dissension soon broke out in the national committee, which voted 18–10 to withdraw its support for the bill. [19]

Another goal of the National Child Labor Committee was to create a federal children's bureau, which would be able to collect information on child labor and other topics related to child welfare and children's rights. The struggle to pass a bill creating such an agency began in the early twentieth century and gained momentum after the first White House Conference on the Care of Dependent Children in 1909. Roosevelt added his endorsement to the bill. Despite strong public support and enthusiasm, however, there were child-helping agencies that opposed the bill, notably, the New York SPCC. Southerners opposed it because they saw it as another step in the effort to regulate child labor. Speaking for the SPCC, Elbridge Gerry labeled the bill to create a federal children's bureau "a dangerous one" and complained that "practically it creates an additional department of the United States Government for the purpose of dictating to States the laws they should pass for their own government on the subject of their children." Answering the SPCC, Lillian Wald suggested that the primary motivation of Gerry and the SPCC was a fear that their work and prerogatives might be threatened. [20]

The bill to create the bureau passed Congress early in 1912 and was signed into law by President Taft in April of that year. The U.S. Children's Bureau, housed in the Department of Commerce and Labor, was charged with investigating and reporting on "all matters pertaining to the welfare of children and child life among all classes of our people, and shall especially investigate the questions of infant mortality, the birth rate, orphanage, juvenile courts, desertion, dangerous occupations, accidents and diseases of children, employment, legislation affecting children in the several States and Territories." Because of concern about the impact of the new law on families, the act prohibited Children's Bureau agents from entering a home without permission. [21]

The National Child Labor Committee meanwhile continued its educational efforts. Opposition to child labor laws, and in particular to federal child labor legislation, was concentrated in the South, where work in the mills had become a way of life in some regions. According to a government report published in 1910:

> For varying reasons the small farmers leave the farm and move to the mill village. Some have been unsuccessful as farmers. Some have been disheartened by poor crops or low prices. . . .
>
> The Personnel of the family often accounts for migration from the farm to the cotton mill. The widow with children too young for farm work readily seizes the opportunity for her children to help in the support of the family at lighter work. The father who is disabled is also easily induced to bring his family from the farm to the mill where he can get the benefit of his children's labor.[22]

The mill owners encouraged workers to bring their children into the factory, even sometimes requiring newly hired workers to agree to bring their children as a condition of employment.[23]

To document the conditions in the mill towns, the national committee hired Lewis Hine to make a photographic record. According to Walter Trattner, Hine would go anywhere: "factories, sheds, mines and homes by night or day, to photograph and interview working children." Hine "secretly measured children's height according to the buttons on his coat, and scribbled notes while keeping his hands in his pockets." When Hine was barred from "the factories and mines, he stayed outside until closing time and took pictures of youngsters as they left work. He also persuaded suspicious mothers to let him photograph birth certificates and records from family bibles." What made Hine vital for the campaign against child labor was that "his pictures were obvious proof of shameful child labor practices."[24]

The reception to the photographs of Lewis Hine, together with the creation of the U.S. Children's Bureau, pointed to a broad shift in public opinion in favor of the regulation of child labor. Indeed, child labor legislation became an issue in the presidential campaign of 1912, with Roosevelt favoring national child labor legislation and Wilson opposing it.

A dramatic event that also aroused public sentiment was the infamous fire at the Triangle Shirtwaist Company in New York in March 1911. Over 140 people died in the fire, most of them young women and girls. A newspaper account conveyed the extent of the tragedy:

> Before smoke or flame gave signs from the windows, the loss of life was fully under way. The first signs that persons in the streets below knew that these three top stories had turned into red furnaces in which human creatures were being incinerated was when screaming men and women and boys and girls

crowded out on the many window ledges and threw themselves into the streets far below.

They jumped with their clothing ablaze. The hair of some of the girls streamed up aflame as they leaped. Thud after thud sounded on the pavements. It is a ghastly fact that on both the Greene Street and Washington Place sides of the building there grew mounds of the dead and dying.

And the worst horror of all was that in this heap of the dead now and then there stirred a limb or sounded a moan.

The fire completely engulfed the top three floors of the building, and many died trying to reach the only fire escape, which could be reached only by climbing through a small window. The impact of this incident was dramatic; like the Hine photographs, it stimulated public support for factory regulation and child labor laws.[25]

The national committee had backed down from endorsing the Beveridge bill on federal regulation of child labor, but early in the second decade of the twentieth century the committee reversed itself and concluded that it should support federal regulation. A delegation called on President Wilson and left an argument for the constitutionality of a federal child labor bill. Wilson agreed not to oppose child labor legislation. The original bill, drafted with the assistance of the National Child Labor Committee, passed the House by a wide margin but did not come to a vote in the Senate. In the next session, the congressional committee draft, by then known as the Keating-Owen bill, passed both houses of Congress in September 1916.

The irony of the Keating-Owen Act was that Wilson received most of the credit for its passage, but his support had come only when political necessity required it. According to Edward Keating, Wilson lent his support at the last minute because 1916 was an election year and the Republicans had claimed that the Democrats would sacrifice child labor to the interests of southern mill owners.[26]

The task of enforcing the law fell to the Labor Department, which assigned it to the Children's Bureau. A special child labor division, headed by Grace Abbott, was created. The National Child Labor Committee stood ready to assist the Children's Bureau, but the chief of the bureau, Julia Lathrop, felt that it should avoid the appearance of being too close to a private agency.[27]

The Southern Cotton Manufacturers Association prepared a case to challenge the new federal law in the summer of 1917. Known as *Hammer* v. *Dagenhart,* the case moved quickly from the original North Carolina trial court, where the child labor law was declared unconstitutional, to the U.S. Supreme Court. The court found in a 5–4 decision handed down in 1918 that Keating-Owen was indeed unconstitutional, on the grounds that Congress had exceeded its authority in attempting to regulate child labor by relying on the interstate commerce clause. The majority opinion held that

in our view the necessary effect of this act is, by means of a prohibition against the movement in interstate commerce of ordinary commercial commodities, to regulate the hours of labor of children in factories and mines within the States, a purely state authority. Thus the act in a twofold sense is repugnant to the Constitution. It not only transcends the authority delegated to Congress over commerce but also exerts a power as to a purely local matter to which the federal authority does not extend.

Justice Oliver Wendell Holmes entered a vigorous dissent for the minority, arguing that there were no limits on the powers of Congress, as argued in the majority opinion.[28]

Opponents of child labor and members of the National Child Labor Committee were shocked by the Court's decision, and a movement to pass a new law began almost immediately. This time Congress passed the Pomerine Amendment, which placed an excise tax on products manufactured with child labor. Again a challenge appeared almost immediately. In the case of *Bailey* v. *Drexel Furniture Co.* the law was declared unconstitutional by the U.S. District Court in western North Carolina and was then appealed to the Supreme Court. In 1922 the Court struck down the second child labor law by a vote of 8–1.[29] In the Court's opinion (written by Chief Justice William Howard Taft), "The provisions of the so called taxing act must be naturally and reasonably adapted to the collection of the tax and not solely to the achievement of some other purpose plainly within state power."[30]

Times had changed; the progressive impulse that brought President Woodrow Wilson around to the cause of child labor seemed to have dissipated during World War I. Congress did pass the Sheppard-Towner Act, designed to lower infant mortality, but did so out of fear of the newly enfranchised female electorate. New ideas, including the notion of a constitutional amendment to prohibit child labor, appeared, but the National Child Labor Committee would have to pursue them without the high level of popular support it had enjoyed before the war.

One new idea was that perhaps child labor could be prevented if some way could be found to keep children out of factories other than through direct legislation. If children could be compelled to be in school during certain hours of the day and during certain periods of the year, they could not be in factories. If children could not be in factories, the temptation to hire children at low wages might lessen. And if there was less interest in hiring children, perhaps child labor would diminish—not by being prohibited but by being discouraged indirectly.

Massachusetts passed the first compulsory school attendance law in 1852; the last state to pass such a law was Mississippi in 1918. Of course, the laws varied in enforcement powers, and the quality of education provided also varied widely. But these laws and a changing social climate did have a profound effect on the incidence of child labor. According to the 1920 census, the number of working children between the ages of 10 and 15 was just over 1 million. In 1910 the number had been twice as high. State child labor laws and compulsory school attendance laws can be credited with most of the decline, but other changes in the work force also lessened the demand for child labor.[31]

Having failed twice in their efforts to regulate child labor through federal legislation, child labor reformers, beginning in 1922, sought passage of a constitutional amendment. The amendment found strong support from the Children's Bureau and organized labor, but it was strongly opposed by factory owners and an assortment of others, including the prominent Boston philanthropist Joseph Lee (who was a leader in the playground movement) and William Cardinal O'Connell, archbishop of Boston. The most vigorous opposition often came from farmers. By 1925 it was clear that the amendment idea had failed; even in progressive states like Massachusetts the amendment was voted down.

The effort to regulate child labor at the federal level continued even after the defeat of the constitutional amendment. As the nation settled into the depths of the Great Depression, the anti–child labor amendment appeared to gain new life when a number of state legislatures ratified it. The reason for this reappearance was the growing incidence of child labor as a consequence of the depression. In the early days of the New Deal, in 1933, the National Recovery Administration (NRA) sought to regulate child labor through the use of codes regulating labor relations in various industries. The government also adopted a temporary "blanket" code for use in all industries that prohibited the employment of children under 16. The prohibition of child labor became a standard feature of virtually all industrial codes adopted during the early New Deal.[32]

Once again, however, the Supreme Court weighed in against the federal regulation of child labor. In 1935, in the case of *Shechter Poultry*

Corporation v. *United States,* the Court found that the National Industrial Recovery Act (which established the NRA) was unconstitutional. The net effect of this ruling, according to the Children's Bureau and the National Child Labor Committee, was a new rise in the employment of children. In 1936 the Children's Bureau interviewed about 2,000 children and concluded that

all left regular day school and had been employed within the month previous to the interview in industrial, commercial, and service occupations (exclusive of agriculture, domestic service, and street trades). . . .

Of the children under 16 years of age, 33 percent were engaged in delivery service, 28 percent were semiskilled production workers, 16 percent were salespersons, and the remaining 23 percent were scattered over a wide variety of other occupations. The 16- and 17-year-old workers, on the other hand, were most often employed as semiskilled production workers. . . . Only a very few of the young workers in each age group were employed in professional or clerical pursuits or in skilled trades, even as learners or helpers.

The Children's Bureau study also found long working hours, dangerous working conditions, and very low wages.[33]

The *Shechter* case revived even more interest in the child labor amendment, which also received an endorsement from President Franklin D. Roosevelt:

One of the accomplishments under the National Recovery Act which has given me the greatest satisfaction is the outlawing of child labor. It shows how simply a long desired reform, which no individual or State could accomplish alone, may be brought about when people work together. It is my desire that the advances attained through N.R.A. be made permanent. In the child labor field the obvious method of maintaining the present gains is through the ratification of the Child Labor Amendment. I hope this may be achieved.[34]

Most Americans probably supported a child labor amendment by 1936, but state legislatures did not move quickly. The overwhelming popularity of the idea, however, did lead to renewed federal action.

The Roosevelt administration combined a child labor provision with minimum wage and maximum hours legislation (in order to get the wage and hours provision passed) in the Fair Labor Standards bill. The action, supported by strong public sentiment, passed Congress in 1938. This act prohibited the employment of children under 16 in industries engaged in interstate commerce and young people under 18 in dangerous occupations. Like its predecessors, it, too, faced a court challenge. But in the case of *United States* v. *Darby* in 1941, the U.S. Supreme Court found the Fair Labor Standards Act constitutional.[35]

The Fair Labor Standards Act did not eliminate all child labor, but it placed the federal government firmly behind the idea that child labor was a social evil that required federal legislation and supervision. The act thus made a clear statement of public policy even if it did not entirely eliminate a clear social wrong.

Conclusion

The most significant development in the history of children's rights in the early twentieth century was the entry of the federal government into the social arena as a vigorous and active player. Early in the twentieth century, the government established the U.S. Children's Bureau and began a series of White House conferences on children and youth that called attention to problems affecting children and families and helped to shape both public opinion and public policy. The supporters of federal regulation of child labor tried at least three times before they achieved a successful federal anti–child labor law. With the passage of the Fair Labor Standards Act in 1938, anti–child labor reformers could count on the federal government as a significant force in the effort to eliminate child labor.

What began as the "century of the child" seemed, at least as far as public sentiment and opposition to child labor were concerned, to have lived up to its promise by midcentury. Yet there was an irony in the child labor campaign. Reformers wished to eliminate all forms of child labor, including work in the home and the street trades. Their motivation came from a desire to protect children rather than to empower them or grant them greater rights. To the child labor reformers, children's rights might well have seemed like a notion dreamed up by the southern cotton mill interests to allow them to hire young children without state or federal interference.

Even so, the prohibition of child labor contained a grain of a notion of rights for children: it established the fundamental right for a child to *be* a child. To enter the world of work before one was fully mature and before one had the opportunity to test one's potential in the arena of education was to deny the possibility of great achievement. The American dream of success, based on Jefferson's aristocracy of talents, could no longer countenance child labor.

Chapter Five

Youth on Its Own, 1920–1930

None of the reform efforts of the Progressive Era can be appreciated fully until their impact on children is assessed. This chapter will describe how children were affected by and reacted to progressive efforts to reform and shape their lives. A central question is, how did children define their own lives? Was a concept of "rights" relevant to them?

There were important developments in the 1920s for children (the Sheppard-Towner Act, for example), but some improvements and areas of concern simply continued from the earlier period. For example, more states made education compulsory. Juvenile courts became more active. The mental hygiene movement developed, and William A. Healy and Augusta Bronner began their effort to find the psychological causes of juvenile delinquency at the Juvenile Psychopathic Institute of Chicago.

The importance of the history of psychology to an understanding of the history of children's rights cannot be overemphasized. Very few Americans objected to basic children's rights (the right to life, the right to be free from abuse, the right to grow up, and the right to a start in life), but from psychology came the idea that children also have a right to a healthy emotional life. It has been very difficult for advocates of children's psychological rights to convince the public of their importance because many Americans have seen these claims as being in conflict with the perceived rights of parents.

Nevertheless, by the second decade of the twentieth century children's rights had evolved still further. During the colonial period a child had the right to life, to a start in life, and to a place in society as an adult, but lacked any right to an "improved" life per se. In the nineteenth century children's right to an education and claim to a decent environment free from abuse began to be recognized. Still later Americans came to believe that children deserve good health and decent living conditions. In the Progressive Era child advocates—adults who sought to better children's lives and life chances—appeared in numbers large enough to be called a movement. The rise of child psychology led to the assertion that a child has a right to growth and development (including psychological growth).

Ironically, the rise of child psychology also led to increased efficiency in the efforts to standardize the lives and experiences of children. As educationists developed standardized tests, children began to be described in terms of the numbers associated with these tests. Standardized tests violated children's privacy and undermined their individuality. Indeed, it can be argued that as we have become more sensitive to rights for children, including the right to individual self-fulfillment, we have increased the amount of regimentation and standardization in children's lives.

The Sheppard-Towner Act

One very bright spot in the 1920s was the Sheppard-Towner Act of 1921. It marked the beginning of government efforts to promote child health with federal funds. The basic idea was to decrease infant mortality in the United States by stressing preventive health care (especially prenatal care for pregnant women). According to Grace Abbott, a pioneer in the field of social work, there were two goals of the Sheppard-Towner Act: "First, to secure an appreciation among women of what constitutes good prenatal and obstetrical care, and second, how to make available adequate community resources so that the women may have the type of care which they need and should be asking for."[1]

Shepphard-Towner provided for the funding of public health nurses to teach parents how to care for children and established clinics where children could receive examinations and mothers could learn about nutrition and sanitation. It also provided for prenatal care and health education for pregnant women. The system set up by the act achieved its goals and is a bench mark for a number of issues—women's roles in health care, the use of the power of the state to improve children's rights, the role of education in issues like infant mortality rates, and the role of physicians in the nation's health care system. After intense lobbying from the American Medical Association (AMA), however, Congress repealed Sheppard-Towner in 1929.[2]

Much of the argument against the act relied on extreme distortion. For example, Sen. James Reed of Missouri, speaking in opposition to a measure to continue Sheppard-Towner, claimed that "the fundamental doctrines on which the bill is founded were drawn chiefly from the radical, socialistic, and bolshevistic philosophy of Germany and Russia." As if this were not enough, Reed also raised the specter of racism in his appeal for southern support for his opposition to the bill.[3] Children had a right to life, it seemed, but only if an M.D. controlled the process.

Children of the Cities

Many of the children who lived in cities in the United States in the early twentieth century spent a great deal of time in the streets. That fact alone worried many of the earnest reformers who sought to improve society by improving the conditions of life for the nation's children. Reformers were horrified at the image of young children working in dangerous factories, but they also worried about the newsboys (and a few newsgirls) and other youthful vendors who could be found on most downtown street corners. They were even more concerned about the messenger boys who worked late at night in the city's worst districts—in saloons, gambling dens, and bordellos.

As if these dangerous occupations were not enough, the reformers also noticed armies of children at play in the streets or patronizing the shops and cheap amusements of the city. To most of the reformers it seemed as if the children of the poor, especially the immigrant poor, were being brought up in the streets. Thus, the reformers sought in a variety of ways literally to get the children off the streets.

Why were the children in the streets? One primary reason was that the streets were interesting; they presented a constantly changing panorama of people and life in action. An observer could learn a great deal about how the city worked (and about life itself) simply by paying attention to what went on in the streets. The streets also represented opportunity: the chance to make some money (and to spend it), to meet friends, to start a game, to socialize or eavesdrop, and to have some fun at the expense of some of the adults who also frequented the streets.

The reformers were appalled by the idea that children were learning not only economics and politics from the streets but also morals. Coming in from the suburbs, these moralists feared for the safety of the street urchins. But as the historian David Nasaw reminds us, "The presence of adults in the street—and in the tenements overhead—protected the children at play." The children "shared their space, but only grudgingly. . . . Their play communities were defined not by their commitment to their own rules but by their disregard for those laid down by adults." In particular, Nasaw writes, "'good' city kids appeared to take special delight in disobeying 'No Swimming' signs in front of the city's concrete fountains . . . teasing the ice man's horse, and stealing whatever they could find from the trucks and pushcarts that invaded their territory."[4] The children resented the intrusion of adults into their play space, but when they were selling something they eagerly sought out the adults as customers.

Children negotiated with some adults, taunted others, and tried to avoid the police, who would not cooperate with their efforts to make the street their space. With the advent of the juvenile court and a new definition of juvenile delinquency, children found themselves arrested for a variety of "status offenses": activities that would not have been treated as crimes if the perpetrators were adults. The enforcement of status offenses meant that children lost some rights even as the reformers sought to protect them from the evils of an industrializing, expanding society.

If the children lost some rights to the courts and the police, they had their own notions of rights as well. They viewed the street as "a separate world with its own standards of right and wrong, its own code of ethics." Despite what children learned in school, at home, and on the streets, they "observed that lots of kids shot craps or pitched pennies, that stealing from the railroads was as common an afternoon's occupation as stickball, that money was for spending, and that your primary duty was to friends, family and fellow gang members—not the police or the laws they claimed to enforce." Finally, on the streets "the children took care of one another. They managed their own space and their own games—according to their own rules."[5]

Thus, children not only had rights that all of society could agree to (though not as many as adult white males), but they also had rights and responsibilities within their own world. They had a right to equal treatment, if they followed the rules, and they could expect loyalty from their friends, provided that they were also loyal. In living and playing in the streets, then, the children learned how society actually worked, and they learned that the people who claimed to be acting in their interest could deprive them of some rights and a considerable amount of freedom.

Psychology and Rights: An Uneasy Alliance

William A. Healy, a respected physician, became the director of the Juvenile Psychopathic Institute in 1909. Jane Addams explained that the institute would attempt to find the causes of juvenile delinquency in individual cases and then seek a course of treatment to remedy the problem. By 1915 Healy had published *The Individual Delinquent,* a handbook for juvenile workers based on the cases that had been referred to the institute. In a somewhat disappointed tone, Healy reported that there was no single causative factor or theory that explained the origins of juvenile delinquency. Rather, he noted, each case was unique, and thus he could suggest only various "causes" such as "bad companions," "mental conflicts," and "love of adventure."[6]

In the following year Healy and his assistant, Augusta F. Bronner, presented a paper on youthful offenders that stressed the need for a holistic approach to the problem of delinquency. They concluded that "our whole work shows nothing more certainly than that no satisfactory study of delinquents, even for practical purposes can be made without building sanely upon the foundations of *all* that goes to make character and conduct."[7]

Ironically, Healy and Bronner's commonsense approach to the study of delinquents may well have contributed to the growth of a juvenile justice system that recognized almost no legal limitations on its powers. The court as an institution prided itself on applying individual remedies to individual delinquents. In effect, the juvenile court took pride in denying due process to the young people who came before it.

In *Mental Conflicts,* published in 1917, Healy found that "mental analysis" (Healy's version of psychoanalysis) needed to be added to the holistic approach to juvenile delinquency. Of 2,000 cases studied, Healy found 147 "instances where mental conflict was a main cause of the delinquency." This finding did not cause him to abandon the holistic approach; instead, he broadened his views to include early family life as a causative factor. "Parental relationship," he concluded, "is so vitally connected with the emotional life of childhood [that] the suggestion of irregularity in it comes as a grave psychic shock."[8]

Healy's findings mark the beginning of society's use of a powerful combination on the family and the lives of children: child science and the juvenile justice (or family court) system. The faith in science as a solution to social problems continued during the 1920s even as enthusiasm for social reform faded. According to a recent scholar, "Professional child-savers believed that science could unlock the secrets of human life, that professional expertise was the highest authority in organized child-saving, and that the many different groups in the American population had to be brought to national standards of health, nutrition, education, and socialization."[9]

Healy had claimed the mantle of science for his version of psychoanalysis, but center stage in the psychological arena of the 1920s belonged to the test-and-measure branch of American psychology. Psychological testing began in earnest in the United States after the introduction of the Binet intelligence test in 1910. Notable among American psychometricians was the educational psychologist Edward L. Thorndike. "Whatever exists, exists in some amount," Thorndike wrote. "To measure it is simply to know its varying amounts."[10] More significant—because he pioneered in the use of the Binet test—was Henry H. Goddard, director of research at New Jersey's Vineland Training School for Feebleminded Boys and Girls. Goddard used the Binet test to classify the inmates at Vineland at different levels. He contended that some mentally deficient people, whom he called morons, were a genuine danger to society because they appeared to be normal and could only be diagnosed if they got into trouble or were measured by an expert. Goddard is best known for his book *The Kallikak Family,* which traced the heredity of "good" and "bad" descendants of one Martin Kallikak, Sr. The point of this melodramatic exercise was to emphasize the need for accurate measurement of predetermined types.[11]

In 1918 Goddard moved from Vineland to the Ohio Bureau of Juvenile Research, where, with his assistant Florence Mateer, he began a testing program that led them to conclude that most mentally deficient young people could be helped and returned to a normal life, provided they received adequate psychotherapy. Thus, they confirmed an early ideal of the progressive juvenile reformers: that delinquents (and by extension, all troubled young people) needed treatment rather than judgment and punishment. Consequently, children who came before the law would be dealt with according to a medical model of social pathology. This had been a central idea when the juvenile court was created. But the work of Healy and Bronner, and later that of Goddard and Mateer, gave the idea the imprimatur of "science."

The potential undermining of children's rights by the combination of science and juvenile justice was under way by the beginning of the 1920s. If testing were in fact as simple as Thorndike and Goddard implied, then juvenile justice authorities, armed with an intelligence test and a scale, could permanently label any young person who came within their grasp. Having done so, they could then prescribe the appropriate "treatment" without reference to any procedural "rights" the child might have, or to any "rights" parents might have either.

A countertrend among child scientists helped to defuse some of that potential. The Iowa Child Welfare Research Station, created by the Iowa legislature in response to the efforts of Cora Bussey Hillis, had as its director of research Bird T. Baldwin, who, unlike Goddard, focused his efforts primarily on the normal child. He contended that children were much more complex than the psychometricians had supposed. According to Hamilton Cravens, what made Baldwin important was that he and his associates "had provided a fresh model of child psychology," which was itself important because it "could be, and was, used to attack both biological determinism and the kind of mental testing determinism that . . . leaders of the psychometric movement championed."[12] Thus, the effort to define a normal child restored a measure of balance to the field of child science and kept it from being confined to Goddard's typology of juvenile pathology. Baldwin's work also confirmed Healy and Bronner's holistic approach to juvenile psychopathology: Healy and Bronner knew that delinquents are complex individuals, and now Baldwin was reminding everyone that all children are complex. Perhaps the danger of psychological labeling had been averted.

To this list of the founders of the holistic view of the normal child the name of Arnold Gesell should be added. Gesell, a student of G. Stanley Hall, saw children as passing through stages of maturation and believed that "normal" did not describe an "average" child but rather one living up to his or her potentialities.[13]

If being normal is a matter of living up to one's potential, then the danger of not doing so is very real. Parents who were conscious of the need for a child to attain his or her potential felt compelled to seek the best possible advice from the most reliable experts. Failing to consult and rely on child-rearing experts was to doom children to abnormality. Thus, the impact of psychology on children's rights was somewhat contradictory: on the one hand, psychologists declined to categorically join the juvenile justice system and thereby conspire to deprive young people of their procedural rights; but on the other hand, psychology did begin to articulate a new right for children—the right to live up to one's potential—the enforcement of which led to considerable coercion and intrusion into the lives of young people.

Mobilizing the Experts

The principal agency for creating and marketing expertise on child rearing in the 1920s and after was the Laura Spelman Rockefeller Memorial. (One could also argue that the U.S. Children's Bureau was a major factor in doing the same thing.) Created in 1918 by John D. Rockefeller with an endowment of $73 million as a memorial to his wife, the organization turned its attention to child study and parent education in 1923 with the appointment of Lawrence K. Frank as director of child study. Like most of the progressives, Frank had a strong faith in science, and he believed that child science could be applied to social problems directly through the technique of parent education. The first task in this endeavor was to foster the growth of child science. Once an adequate base of child science became available, then scientifically based parent education could proceed. Such a course would fulfill the progressive promise to transform society and cure the twin ills of industrialization and urbanization.[14]

Other agencies also supported the idea of parent education. The National Congress of Parents and Teachers (an outgrowth of the National Congress of Mothers) had long favored the development of some kind of scientific basis for the institution of motherhood. The National Congress had appeared in 1897 at the instigation of Mrs. Theodore (Alice McLellan) Birney. By 1920 it had 190,000 members in 36 states. One of its earliest efforts was developing courses in "domestic science" in high schools and colleges for young women. As Mrs. Birney explained, "As soon as the men and women of America are fully awake to the dangers to which their ignorance gives rise, there will be such appreciation of the rights of children to be well born, wisely bred and trained, as will place parenthood where it justly belongs as the *highest of all vocations.*"[15] Where Mrs. Birney wanted educated motherhood and thus advocated college for women, Lawrence Frank wanted first a specific kind of child science and then a means of applying that science directly to children.

Frank lent support to child study activities in Iowa, at Yale, and at the University of Minnesota and the University of California at Berkeley. The Minnesota Institute of Child Welfare secured a faculty, engaged in research, and established parent training centers across the state. But it was in Iowa that Frank established the first statewide parent education program. More significantly, perhaps, Frank and the Rockefeller Memorial helped create a professional climate for psychologists and others who worked in child psychology. He was aided by the efforts of Robert

S. Woodworth, a Columbia psychologist who persuaded the Rockefeller Memorial to fund the creation of a professional subculture. In 1927, for example, that organization began supporting the publication of *Child Development Abstracts and Bibliography*.[16]

Two other trends during the twenties—a period of great expansion in the social sciences—would prove important to the growth of child advocacy: the promotion of child guidance and the growth of professional child psychiatry. Funded by money from the Commonwealth Fund of New York, the National Committee for Mental Hygiene developed and fostered interest in mental hygiene, particularly as a means of preventing juvenile delinquency. This development led in time to the child guidance movement, which sought to prevent delinquency by applying expertise to normal children.

Thus, in the 1920s several different professions focused on children. Everyone's goal was to promote healthy, psychologically sound children who would become successful, productive adults. Child scientists would develop the expertise parents needed, and child psychiatry would supply guidance counselors to aid the efforts of the parents. Parent education, school counselors, and when these two parties failed, the courts, all stood ready to weigh in on behalf of the child. The net effect of all these efforts was to refine the concept of children's rights—the right "to be well born, wisely bred and trained," in Mrs. Birney's words—in such a way as to define most homes and families as pathological. According to historian Christopher Lasch, "Doctors, psychiatrists, teachers, child guidance experts, officers of the juvenile courts, and other specialists began to supervise child-rearing, formerly the business of the family."[17] This development left the question of the actual rights of children in a state of confusion. Consider, for example, the following comments from Dr. Douglas A. Thom, a Boston psychiatrist writing in 1922:

The home represents the workshop in which . . . personalities are being developed, and the mental atmosphere of the home can be very easily contaminated. The ever-changing moods of the parents, colored by their indifference, their quarrels, depressions, and resentments, and shown by their manner of speech and action, are decidedly unhealthy; so, too, are the timidity of a mother, the arrogance of a father, the self-consciousness of a younger sister, and the egotism of an older brother. Under such conditions we find a mental atmosphere as dangerous to the child as if it were contaminated by scarlet fever, diptheria, or typhoid.[18]

The antidote to this pathology was, of course, massive intervention in a variety of forms. In the 1920s Miriam Van Waters observed that when experts diagnosed a child as defective or epileptic, the parents became despondent. "Such observations," Christopher Lasch notes, "seldom prompt those who made them to question the wisdom of professional teaching." The trouble, according to Lasch, was the idea of "a norm of child development, deviations from which necessarily give rise to parental alarm, to further demands for professional intervention, and often to measures that intensify suffering instead of alleviating it."[19]

Flaming Youth and Rights: The Rise of the Peer Group

The 1920s was the decade when young people came into prominence in American society. According to historian Paula Fass, "In the 1920s, youth appeared suddenly, dramatically, even menacingly on the social scene." The rise of youth "signaled a social transformation of major proportions"; Fass contends that "they were a key to the many changes which had remade society."[20]

Adolescence itself was changing. Young men who could afford higher education knew that successful completion of college assured them a place in America's expanding economy. Young women began to claim the same right to education their brothers had. By leaving home for college or for work, girls gained an enormous amount of personal freedom.

One symbol of this new freedom was the rise of dating, which replaced courtship and in the process also replaced chaperonage. Young people themselves created and maintained the rules of conduct for dating and a whole series of social relationships. Dating arose in part out of necessity, as historian Beth Bailey explains: "Dating stemmed originally from the lack of opportunities. Calling, or even just visiting, was not a practicable system for young people whose families lived crowded into one or two rooms." Thus, for many young women, "the parlor and the piano often simply did not exist."[21] The system of dating spread rapidly across the country in the 1920s and gave rise to a different set of social relations between young people.

The date represented a kind of bargain: boys paid, girls granted some degree of intimacy. Rules established by the peer group defined the limits and the timing of the relaxation of those limits. In a recent study, John Modell concludes that "girls had more to gain by the establishment of dating, because the new version of the double standard that it put into place was considerably less restrictive to them than the one it replaced." Dating broadened the range of young men the girls might meet, and it gave them more freedom to explore and experiment. [22]

Dating customs and adolescent peer groups may seem irrelevant to the subject of rights for children, particularly legal rights. But if rights are considered in terms of what a person may reasonably claim for herself or himself, then the rise of both dating and peer groups is very significant. Young people of the 1920s were at once more liberated than previous generations and more conforming. Peer groups enforced strict rules of conduct and codified the process of rebellion against adult authority. At the same time, peer groups made it safe for young people to experiment in their behavior, including their sexual behavior, and to learn more about members of the opposite sex through dating relationships. Thus, young people were free from close adult supervision of some parts of their lives, but to gain this freedom they had to sacrifice some elements of individuality to their peers. In addition, all was not equal within peer groups; status depended upon such qualities as wealth, personal appearance, social background, and conformity to group rules. [23]

The rise of peer groups in the 1920s provided middle-class young people with greater control over their own lives, particularly in the areas of sexual exploration, social adjustment, and entry into modern white-collar life. According to Modell, "The 1920s promoted the emergence of our modern youthful life course, normatively sanctioned for the middle class, spreading among other urbanites." The main feature of this life course was a combination of "extended schooling" and "an early and gradual peer-structured courtship system," which tended to promote "an early and often romantic marriage." [24] Modell believes this development was responsible for a break between generations and a greater tendency for new families to be separated both emotionally and geographically from their families of origin.

Conclusion

By the 1920s children's rights had reached a certain peak. This decade did not witness any expansion in individual rights for excluded groups in society, but it did create structures that gave young people, especially young women, more personal freedom. That freedom over their own lives, a new personal autonomy within well-defined limits, represented a net gain for young people, but it came at the high price of surrendering to the authority of the peer group. And not all groups acquired this autonomy: only the middle class participated effectively in peer societies in high school and college.

Child psychology expanded dramatically in the 1920s; the developing expertise in this field would ultimately add a psychological dimension to the question of rights for children. Because of eventual public acceptance of child science, by the late twentieth century it was commonly accepted that all children deserved not only rights to life, growth, freedom from abuse, and a start in life, but also the right to sound conditions for healthy psychological development. The expansion of this sphere of the helping professions was thus a major accomplishment of the 1920s. Ironically, the growth of child science, which would broaden the claims of children in the future, also narrowed the legal and procedural rights of children before the bar of justice. Armed with "truths" from the realm of psychology, the juvenile justice system could use its formidable power to limit the freedom and rights of young people it found to be either endangered or delinquent. Experts also used psychology to standardize the lives and experiences of children. The rise of standardized tests in particular led to the stereotyping of children and to the systematic violation of children's privacy.

A bright spot in the 1920s was the Sheppard-Towner Act. A remarkable success, the act showed what could be accomplished through education. If the most basic right a child has is the right to life, then the Sheppard-Towner Act represented a major commitment on the part of the U.S. government to that basic right. The destruction of Sheppard-Towner by conservative interests, led by the American Medical Association, was one of the most grievous blows American children have ever received. The long-term consequence of the destruction of Sheppard-Towner has been an infant mortality rate in the United States higher than that of any other industrialized country in the world. Although children's rights and the number and type of child advocates has continued to expand since the 1920s, a central fact that cannot be ignored is that the United States, so far as the health of infants is concerned, remains an underdeveloped country.

Eight-year-old girl working in a Georgia cotton mill, 1909. *Lewis Hine #545, Photography Collections, University of Maryland, Baltimore County*

Boys at Amoskeag Mills, Manchester, New Hampshire, 1909. *Lewis Hine #814, Photography Collections, University of Maryland, Baltimore County*

Boys at the Ewen Breaker, Pennsylvania, 1911. *Lewis Hine #1941, Records of the Children's Bureau, National Archives*

Japanese child awaiting internment, 1942. *Relocation Authority, National Archives*

Evicted tenant farmers near Sikeston, Missouri, January 1939. Memphis Commercial Appeal, *Mississippi Valley Collection, Brister Library, Memphis State University*

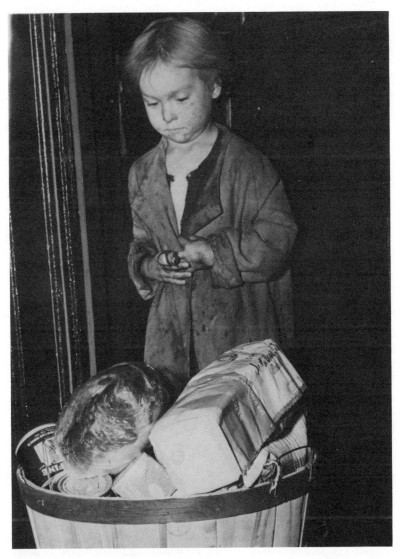

Relief food, Memphis, Tennessee, 4 December 1938. Memphis Commercial Appeal, *Mississippi Valley Collection, Brister Library, Memphis State University*

The face of poverty, Memphis, Tennessee, 18 June 1951. Memphis Commercial Appeal, *Mississippi Valley Collection, Brister Library, Memphis State University*

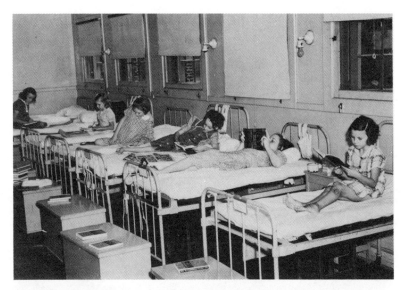

Hospital for crippled children, Memphis, Tennessee, 20 September 1941. Memphis Commercial Appeal, *Mississippi Valley Collection, Brister Library, Memphis State University*

Teaching mentally retarded child to buy groceries, Memphis, Tennessee, May 1955. Memphis Commercial Appeal, *Mississippi Valley Collection, Brister Library, Memphis State University*

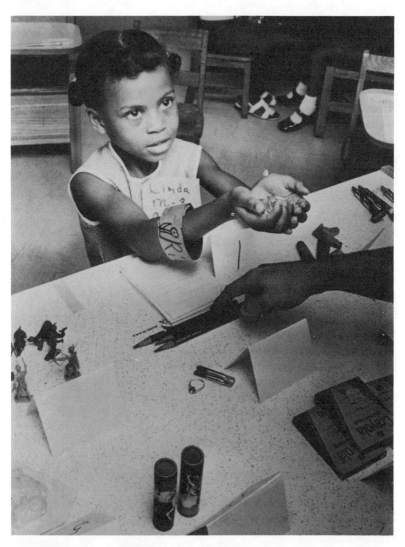

Head-start participant receiving immediate reward for good performance, Memphis, Tennessee, July 1969. Memphis Commercial Appeal, *Mississippi Valley Collection, Brister Library, Memphis State University*

Children at play, Eastside Elementary School, Memphis, Tennessee, 1971. Memphis Commercial Appeal, *Mississippi Valley Collection, Brister Library, Memphis State University*

Chapter Six

The Establishment of Government Programs for Children, 1930–1940

Both progress and decline characterize the 1930s so far as children's rights are concerned. The defeat of the Sheppard-Towner Act was a major setback for the advocates of a federally-funded health care program. Nonetheless, the act would set a precedent for large federal programs for children in the period after World War II. Although the prenatal preventive program under Sheppard-Towner did not continue because of the opposition of the American Medical Association, concern for the health of children did not wither away. Much of the major legislation of the New Deal, such as the Social Security and Fair Labor Standards acts, focused directly on children, was intended to improve children's lives, and extended the range or domain of rights children might claim.

An army of adults concerned about the nation's future and therefore very much aware of the circumstances and needs of the nation's children, coalesced into a movement in the 1930s. These child advocates included social workers, juvenile court staff, teachers, parents, staffers at the U.S. Children's Bureau, public health nurses, volunteer workers with children, and other civic-minded folk. The hard times of the depression made them more receptive to the idea that investment in youth was one area that should be protected if possible. (Social investment is a difficult concept to grasp in the late twentieth century, when resistance to taxes and social programs seems to be at an all-time high.) The child advocates pushed for federal action on behalf of children, and much of the credit for the laws benefiting children passed in this decade must go to them.

But the depression was harmful to children as well. Infant mortality rates rose. The material circumstances of children, documented in numerous studies but never more grippingly than by the Farm Security Administration (FSA) photographers, declined dramatically. Children were pressed into jobs when parents could not find work. Rural children, though not employed for wages, worked long hours at difficult and dangerous tasks. Schools suffered as well. Sometimes teachers could not be paid; schools closed or held double sessions and put off maintenance for better times. Other services, such as the clinics established under Sheppard-Towner, disappeared or were curtailed. Diets changed—children no longer ate as well as they had, nor did pregnant women. People accepted what they had to for housing and clothing. Some lost homes and farms and took up a migrant life.

The New Deal focused on children and youth in a number of ways. The premise of Sheppard-Towner—that the federal government would actively promote better living conditions for some of the people—paved the way for the creation of new agencies and the passing of legislation that enabled further direct government assistance and additional intrusion of the government into the lives of ordinary citizens. Thus, child advocates could look to the federal government to improve conditions for children across the entire nation. The New Deal did not establish new rights for children in the sense that new ideas appeared and were accepted; instead, many old ideas about the rights of children finally received federal guarantees. All could agree that children deserved a basic start in life; now children could claim that right with the backing of the federal government if necessary. But the claim has been limited by the persistence of another American value: self-reliance.

During the New Deal the United States established a national welfare system. It was and is a system that stigmatizes recipients. In the name of helping children, it has confined recipients to the lowest rungs of society and the least desirable housing while removing all semblance of dignity from the family. The notion of children's rights seems surreal when mothers must beg for the most basic necessities for their children, while living in neighborhoods where drugs and drug dealing seem to offer the only escape. But the planners and dreamers of the thirties could not foresee the often tragic consequences of their labors; they saw the misery of hard times and meant only to improve the situation.

To understand the children's rights movement in late twentieth–century America, it is necessary to first understand how the federal government came to dominate the arena of social welfare. We need to appreciate the impact of the depression on thinking about public policy in the United States and on individual lives. The New Deal, its origins, its efforts to remedy the defects of the American system, and the results and implications of those efforts provided the backdrop for the emergence of a new national coalition of child advocates.

The Great Depression

It is difficult to imagine the impact of the Great Depression on Americans' lives, even with the numbers at hand. Steel plants operated at 12 percent of capacity. Industrial construction declined from $949 million to $74 million between 1929 and 1932, by which time unemployment had reached 13 million. Famine and homelessness became commonplace.[1] In some cities people lived in ramshackle shacks known ironically as "Hoovervilles." As one survivor recalled: "I knew one family there in Oklahoma City, a man and a woman and seven children lived in a hole in the ground. You'd be surprised how nice it was, how nice they kept it. They had chairs and tables, and beds back in that hole. And they had the dirt all braced up there, just like a cave."[2]

Children first became aware of the depression when their family's fortunes obviously fell. Some families disintegrated, but others drew closer together. As Robin Langston of Hot Springs, Arkansas, recalls, "I knew the Depression had really hit when the electric lights went out." Sometimes children found work and contributed to the family economy. Children worked as newspaper carriers, baby-sitters, messengers, clerks, whatever they could find. Older children worked for the National Youth Administration (NYA), a New Deal agency.[3]

In a massive study of the impact of the depression on family life, *Children of the Depression,* Glen Elder followed up on a study of 167 preadolescent children in Oakland, California, begun in 1931. Elder wished to know what impact the loss of income had had on the lives of these children. For example, reduced family circumstances led many children to enter the work force and had a lasting effect on them. According to Elder, "A large number of the study members are convinced that hardship in the Depression has made a difference in their financial outlook." In addition, "they tend to use the Depression as an explanation for their behavior." As one young white-collar worker put it, he had come to "realize that money doesn't always come so easy. It makes you just a little conservative in spending money, especially in spending it beyond your means."[4]

European observers were surprised at the passivity of the unemployed in the United States. Radicalism or mob action seemed to have no place, and even in the election of 1932 the Communists polled only 120,000 votes. Some even came to believe that society itself was disintegrating. The birth rate fell, and pundits saw a dire future if that trend continued: schools would stand empty; markets were shrinking, and the means to recover might never be available.[5]

Under these circumstances, society tended to ignore the voice and interests of children and young people, even though the previous decade had been the age of "flaming youth." Youth symbolized the future and the bright hope of endless economic expansion. At a time when resources and morale were on the decline, the same behavior that had made young people the darlings of society now seemed indulgent and wasteful. Elder found that many children reported a return to basic values as a result of the hard times.

The New Deal

The New Deal was not so much the result of a coherent ideology as a series of specific responses to specific problems or issues. Yet there was a consistency about both the Roosevelt administration's approach to problems and the kinds of problems it addressed. New Dealers distrusted financial experts, relied on centralized planning such as had occurred during the Great War, and focused on social problems in part because so many of them had been either social workers or settlement house residents. Advisers to the Roosevelt administration, popularly known as the Brain Trust, differed in almost all particulars as to what they thought had caused the depression and what might be done about it. They could agree, however, that there were imbalances in the economy, and they saw themselves as working to restore balance. In their minds, the issue was the imbalance between industry and agriculture.

The New Deal was launched during the famous "hundred days" of the first three months of Roosevelt's first term. The specific acts of legislation are less important than the new spirit of activism that flowed from the new administration. Congress moved quickly to deal with a bank crisis, then to placate angry farmers, and then to develop programs for the unemployed and to protect home owners. It was also becoming clear that the federal government would have to take on the enormous task of providing emergency relief to families and individuals who were out of work or who had lost everything in bank failures. Congress created the

Federal Emergency Relief Administration (FERA) in May 1933 and later established the Civil Works Administration to provide jobs for the unemployed. The creation of the Works Progress Administration (WPA) in 1935 was the federal government's largest and most important relief effort.[6]

Two federal efforts pertained directly to children: the creation of the Civilian Conservation Corps (CCC) and the National Youth Administration. The CCC was the first federal relief agency to be established and had a dual purpose: to provide relief for young men and to preserve forest and farm lands and construct public recreation areas. Young men who joined lived in camps run by the army and worked at a variety of conservation tasks. More than 2.5 million young men had enrolled by the time the CCC was disbanded in 1942. The corps was for young men between the ages of 17 and 25 from families on relief. They received $30 a month and were supposed to send most of it home.[7]

Many young men did not join the CCC because of its regimentation, and the CCC offered nothing for young women. To meet the growing needs of young people, Roosevelt created the National Youth Administration by executive order in 1935. It administered four different types of programs for youth aged 16 to 25: work-study for students from families on relief; employment on work projects for those out of school; vocational assistance; and organized recreation. Over 2½ million young people were involved in the work projects during the years of the NYA (1935–43). The NYA tried to serve equal numbers of male and female youth. A first, the agency did little to challenge prevailing stereotypes about gender roles. Young men were more likely to obtain marketable skills through the NYA than young women, and most young women received training in home economics. Both the CCC and the NYA included African-Americans in their programs, but neither agency was immune to racial prejudice. For example, black women found themselves channeled into jobs white women did not want.[8]

In 1939 the NYA began teaching defense-related industrial skills to males. As the draft depleted the ranks of young men, NYA officials extended this training to young women in 1940. Thus, Rosie the Riveter may well have received her training through the NYA. By continuing to emphasize domestic images in its promotional material, the NYA may also have contributed to the expectation that Rosie would go back home after the war was over.

Despite some obvious biases, the NYA dealt more directly with the issue of race than did many other New Deal agencies, partly because of the influence of Mary McLeod Bethune, the founder of Bethune-Cook-man College in Daytona Beach, Florida. She was a member of the NYA advisory committee, which had a division of Negro affairs, and she worked to make sure that young African-Americans received equal services through the NYA. She also worked to publicize the efforts of the Division of Negro Affairs.[9]

In 1938 Mrs. Bethune filed a report with the director of the NYA, Aubrey Williams. After praising what had been accomplished, she pointed out many of the deficiencies in programs for young African-Americans, noting in particular that they did not have equal access to the more desirable programs such as apprenticeship training and the vocational guidance program. She called for a number of improvements, including the idea that the NYA "foster and gain the cooperation of the WPA for the setting up of a curative mecca for crippled Negro children similar to the nationally famous Warm Springs Foundation from which Negroes are barred."[10]

Photographs taken by NYA photographers documented the policies and approaches of the agency. Classes and programs tended to be segregated by sex and race. The photographs portray stereotypical activities; one shows two well-dressed young women "applying delicate tints" to pictures for use in schools. Another shows young black women "filling soup containers with hot beef soup." Some photographs, however, depict young women learning industrial skills, such as welding and machining, and others depict biracial work situations. The latter photographs generated trouble for the agency from conservative southern democrats.[11]

The NYA was ended on an essentially partisan vote in 1943. From its inception it had aided over 600,000 college-aged youth and over 1½ million high school–aged young people through its work-study programs. It also provided skills training and led to the construction or establishment of over 3,000 educational buildings.[12]

Even more far-reaching in its impact than the NYA, especially on children's rights, was social security, which Roosevelt proposed in January 1935. The idea was to create a national system that would remedy some of the defects of existing relief programs. There was little disagreement over creating a national system of old-age and survivor's insurance, but the question of unemployment compensation proved much more difficult. One of the documents used in drafting the legislation, "Security for Children," was a staff study prepared by Katherine F. Lenroot and Martha M. Eliot of the Children's Bureau. Lenroot, who had a background in social work, was chief of the bureau; Eliot, the assistant chief, was a pediatrician and had previously been the director of the bureau's Division of Child and Maternal Health. Both were veterans of federal service; Lenroot had been with the bureau since 1915, and Eliot had joined in 1924.[13]

The Children's Bureau staff study was, in effect, a brief for basic rights for children, especially the right to adequate conditions in which to grow. Lenroot and Eliot contended that

security for families, the broad foundation upon which the welfare of American children must rest, involves economic, health, and social measures which pertain to the entire economic and social structure of our civilization. Among them are an adequate wage level and a reasonable workday and workweek, with provision of regular and full employment necessary to yield a stable and sufficient family income; unemployment insurance or compensation when full employment fails; [and] provision of adequate medical care and promotion of physical and mental health.

They argued that all social security measures were in reality child welfare measures. Old-age pensions, for example, relieved families with children at home of the burden of caring for aged parents. Lenroot and Eliot also identified a new right for children—the right to adequate health care. "All children need health protection," they wrote, "to provide which the community and the State as well as individual parents have a responsibility." The need for social security came also from the shocking realization that 8 million people on relief—40 percent of the total—were children under 16.[14]

While child advocates in the Children's Bureau were arguing for increased federal attention to the needs of children (and Lenroot and Eliot stressed that social security covered only part of the needs of the nation's children), others began to document the social effects of the depression. Notable among them were Robert S. and Helen Merrell Lynd, who focused on Muncie, Indiana, in their famous study *Middletown in Transition* (1937). The Lynds found that Muncie schools pulled young people in opposite directions: they encouraged young people to think for themselves, but to meet the needs of the community, they also stressed the need for sacrifices and lowered ambitions. School officials and teachers seemed overly cautious, perhaps fearing for their jobs. The Lynds thus identified an important dilemma. Everyone could agree that young people had the right to improve themselves and that they were the hope of the future. Still, it was difficult if not impossible to give youth and society the hope they needed.[15]

Robert Lynd had an influential friend in the federal government: Roy Stryker of the Farm Security Administration. Stryker, a veteran of the Union Settlement House in New York City, had attended Columbia University, where he studied with Rexford Guy Tugwell. Later he joined Tugwell at the Resettlement Administration, which later became the FSA, and became chief of its photographic section. Lynd, impressed with the photographs already taken by FSA photographers, convinced Stryker that the FSA could undertake a sociological study of small-town life in the United States, using photography as the principal means of documentation. In the process, FSA photographers, like so many other New Dealers, would become social advocates who illustrated the deprivation of many Americans, including many children.[16]

Children figure prominently in many of the FSA photographs, which recall the significant photographic studies of children by Jacob Riis and Lewis Hine. Like the FSA photographers, Riis and Hine saw themselves as both documenters of the existence of social abuse and advocates of social reform—especially Hine, who worked for the National Child Labor Committee. For the most part, Hine photographed children at work in factories around or on machinery and in the fields lugging huge sacks of cotton. Sometimes he took group shots outside factories and at other times he took portraits. For Hine, the point was context—the dangerous machinery or the drudgery of labor in a cotton field. FSA photographers, by contrast, studied the conditions of life for the nation as a whole and illustrated the fact that the material conditions of life for everyone, children included, were stark. Where Hine took a stereotypical picture of a subject, some of the best of the FSA photographers used their photographs to make eloquent statements. A 1937 Walker Evans photograph of the Bud Fields family in Alabama, for example, includes father, mother, grandmother, and three children, of whom one is a babe in arms. The family is unsmiling, even grim-faced, and the poverty of their surroundings is unmistakable. Probably the most famous photograph of the entire FSA collection is Dorothea Lange's *Migrant Mother,* taken in California in 1936. Two small children stand close by their mother, their faces turned away from the camera. The mother tugs at her cheek with one hand. Unsmiling and serious, she gazes off in the distance. Her clothing and that of her children is worn and ragged. Equally compelling is a Russell Lee shot of four very young children (one stands on a box) eating Christmas dinner in 1936 in southeastern Iowa. All four are focused intently on the bowl of food on the table.[17]

The FSA deliberately put its photographs before the public. They appeared regularly in *Survey Graphic,* a socially conscious magazine owned by the Kellogg family. Some images appeared in camera and photography magazines, some were reproduced in reports published by the FSA, and some were exhibited at photography shows. But most Americans came to know the FSA photographs through books, the two most famous being *American Exodus* by Dorothea Lange and Paul Taylor and *Let Us Now Praise Famous Men* by James Agee and Walker Evans.[18]

On the one hand, Americans came to know the depths and effects of the depression from the numbers they could read in newspapers, magazines, and countless government staff reports. On the other hand, people experienced hard times firsthand, and from the FSA images they could identify themselves and their own conditions. Though hopelessness and despair were dominant themes in these images, there was in the children a glimmer of possibility. Find the means to improve the lives of children, the photographers seemed to be saying, and they might enjoy a better future. Thus, the children of hard times were the hope of the future, and child advocates began to articulate the claims of children in both words and images.

Meanwhile, the federal government, in passing the Social Security Act of 1935, had begun the principal system of social welfare in the United States. In comparison with other industrialized countries, the U.S. social security system was both conservative and niggardly. Many classes of workers, such as domestics and agricultural laborers, were not covered, and many causes of poverty, such as sickness and disability, were not adequately addressed. Yet where rights are concerned, the Social Security Act was a major turning point in American history. The payment of social security taxes gave most working Americans an unassailable claim to social security benefits.[19]

The Social Security Act also established a federal presence in social welfare and inaugurated federal aid to children. At first called Aid to Dependent Children (ADC) (now Aid to Families with Dependent Children [AFDC]), the federal welfare system arose out of the concerns expressed by Lenroot and Eliot in their staff report. The system is administered by states, according to national guidelines. While this section of the Social Security Act established precedent for the right to aid for dependent children, aiding children was not the primary focus of social security legislation, and Congress was in fact relatively uninterested in the provisions pertaining to children. It was an outgrowth of efforts begun early in the century to aid desperate mothers and enable them to keep their children. Most of the states had established mother's aid laws by 1931, but as historian Leroy Ashby observes, "the programs tended to be permissive rather than mandatory, minuscule in coverage, and at the mercy of local politics." In addition, the policies established under this program (in essence, a federal matching program administered by states) prescribed a "suitable home" for children, making aid dependent on the behavior of mothers, who could lose the aid money for a variety of actions, including drunkenness or even inadequate discipline. Thus, the New Deal's development of aid for children continued the age-old practice of requiring deference and loyalty in exchange for minuscule amounts of charity. Though the system seemed to establish a right to support, that right was contingent upon the favors of local officials. The system in effect reduced mothers to the status of beggars and may well have harmed the interests of the children supposedly being protected. Probably no other aspect of the American welfare system occasioned so much debate as did the "suitable home" provision. In later years federal staffers would strive to reduce the oppression generated by this provision and to elevate the claims of dependent children to the status of rights. Eventually the issue would reach the Supreme Court.[20]

Title V of the Social Security Act provided federal grants-in-aid to states for the expansion of services for neglected and abused children, but in some cases little or nothing was done. Under the Federal Emergency Relief Administration, much direct assistance had gone to children (providing shoes and clothing, for example), but in some states there was a delay in creating the program. In Mississippi, for example, no ADC program was established until 1941.[21]

Other New Deal agencies also assisted children. The WPA established nursery schools staffed by unemployed teachers. The FERA and later the WPA provided housekeeping aid to households with children or dependent elderly people. The program was designed not only to help the needy families but also to provide employment to the aides.[22]

Of all the aid programs for children in the 1930s, the day nurseries probably aroused the most public interest and support. Many middle-class families used these schools as day-care centers, thus establishing a precedent for federally funded day-care centers and breaking the old notion that day care was for poor or pathological families only. The need for such services had been made real by the economic circumstances of the depression, but they proved so popular that many families urged their continuation even as the economy improved. In 1936 Edna Ewing Kelley, supervisor of nursery schools in the Texas Department of Education, put the case in terms of the rights and needs of children: "The establishment of free nursery schools in America is a pioneer movement. But the time has come when individuals and communities should catch the vision and feel the responsibility for the educational and physical welfare of all pre-school children. Then and only then, will the free nursery school become a permanent institution in this country."[23]

In its final report the WPA claimed that not only had the nursery schools improved the lives of children because of the medical care and healthful environment, including nutritious meals, that they provided, but they also gave employment to teachers, nurses, dietitians, and other workers.[24]

Day care would become a major political, economic, social, and philo-sophical issue in American society during World War II and after. The strong bias against government interference in families—which historian Elizabeth Pleck has called "the family ideal"—has meant that public sup-port for institutions for children has had to be justified on grounds other than enforcement of some notion of children's rights. The rights of the family, so this view goes, take precedence over any claims children might have. Additionally, any expenditure of public funds must be seen in eco-nomic terms. Thus, the legislation of the New Deal, although it laid down numerous precedents for using the power of the federal government for social ends, did not break new ground so far as new *legal* rights for chil-dren were concerned.

Other Children's Rights Developments in the 1930s

The depression of the 1930s strained the resources of the nation—es-pecially those devoted to social causes and issues. For example, a con-troversy arose over the delivery of protective services for children in New York City. The New York Society for the Prevention of Cruelty to Children had long had police powers granted by the legislature enabling its agents to bring charges of neglect and abuse against adults. The agents who exercised these powers were not required to have any spe-cial qualifications or to undergo any public scrutiny before appointment. An investigation into the political appointment of some of these agents in 1936 led a judge of the domestic relations court of New York, Justine Wise Polier, to complain about the workings of the SPCC. Because the SPCC was private, even its shelters for children were not subject to routine visits from the state's Board of Social Welfare. Judge Polier articulated a subtle but important point: by treating children outside the traditional legal and social mechanisms, Americans had possibly improved their individual situations; but this improvement may have come at the expense of some of the legal rights and guarantees children might otherwise have possessed. Still, replied the American Humane Association—the federation of societies seeking to prevent cruelty to both children and animals—the major purpose of a child protection agency "is the protection of children from cruel abuse and neglect."[25]

On quite a different level, another 1930s event in the history of children's rights was the conclusion of a 1933 panel of academic experts that movies had a very dramatic impact on children, and that much of the content of the movies was inappropriate for children. In particular, they complained about excesses of sex, violence, and crime. The panel's solution was the creation of wholesome and appealing movies especially for children.

Juvenile Delinquency

Even though juvenile delinquency had not been solved, most Americans were satisfied with the system for dealing with it that had been established. The problem certainly did not disappear in the 1930s, and the system itself was far from perfect. Children and youth were still confined with adults in local jails, and the conditions in jails were frequently deplorable.[26]

One reform idea was to create a centralized "youth authority" that would have charge of all juveniles in a state's correctional system. An advocate of such an approach, William A. Healy, who had worked with the Cook County juvenile court early in the century, argued that the system in place did not deter repeat offenders and had been little changed since its inception. The new youth authority model would individualize the treatment of youthful offenders, a venerable idea within juvenile programs. The reformers also believed that statewide administration was critical to such an idea. Critics were alarmed because the new system would threaten or eliminate a juvenile offender's procedural rights. In addition, this new model would undermine one of the oldest ideas in modern criminal justice—the notion that punishment should fit the crime, not the criminal.

The proposed youth authority deeply troubled John Forbes Perkins, a Boston juvenile court judge. He questioned its basic assumptions and suggested that it would impinge on the rights of young people. Children understand the concept of equality under law directly from their own experience, he argued. "The demand for equality under law," he continued, "is not a political slogan nor a metaphysical concept conceived by a philosopher. It is simply the result of what children have found from infinite experience since the beginning of time to be the essential element of living together successfully. It is what we mean by fair play. . . . Liberty is no catch phrase. We don't willingly accept discipline. We are jealous of our independence." Perkins believed that the new approach would substitute "protection" for liberty and equality. [27]

Reformers countered that determinate sentences had not worked, and that they had been based on the idea of punishment rather than the idea of rehabilitation. John Barker Waite, a law professor at the University of Michigan, put the case for the new youth system in practical terms when he noted that it permitted "a wide variety of treatment methods." A juvenile under the control of the youth authority could be placed either in a correctional institution or "in a hospital, in a vocational training or educational institution." Or the youth authority could require the juvenile "to undergo a course of treatment in a mental hygiene or other clinic, or in fact put him [or, presumably, her] in any community situation it may consider helpful." Waite explained that the legal basis for this proposition was similar to that for the commitment of the mentally ill. Thus, in Waite's view, children had the same rights as people with mental incapacities. [28]

Indeterminate sentences and the idea of individualizing the treatment of offenders had been advocated before. Behind these ideas lay one even more appealing—the notion that crime itself could be eliminated if only the right formula, the proper scientific approach, could be found. Efforts to reform juvenile delinquents had begun early in the nineteenth century when reformers thought they could eliminate pauperism (a chronic and debilitating form of poverty, and almost literally a crime) by reforming youthful offenders. Crime itself, they almost promised, would likewise disappear if youthful offenders could be caught early enough and treated in the proper fashion. In 1940 this dream was still alive, but by then the experts believed that the secret was prevention—to catch potential youthful offenders even before they committed an illegal act. The 1940 White House Conference on Children and Youth in a Democracy emphasized the importance of prevention, and the conferees argued, commendably, that many of the stress factors that led to delinquency were economic in origin. But the emphasis in this report was not on improving the economic lot of every American family; rather, it was on nipping youthful misbehavior in the bud before children became full-fledged criminals.[29] Such an approach meant that all children, and especially those from poor homes, were to be under constant scrutiny, an idea hardly compatible with respect for children's rights.

Conclusion

The single most important development in the 1930s so far as children were concerned was the entry of the federal government into the social arena. If the Great Depression made children's lives harder and narrowed the range of opportunities available to them, it led to the New Deal and the passage of a number of laws that eventually improved their lives. The Social Security Act was the most important piece of legislation, and its passage meant that for many young Americans the right to a decent start in life acquired substantive meaning. Similarly, the Fair Labor Standards Act contained *effective,* constitutional, federal child labor regulations. Children had the right to mature, at least in part, before they entered the world of work (see Chapter 4).

These two primary contributions to the lives of children—economic security for some, and freedom from the need to work at an early age— can be called advances in children's rights. The emergence of a large corps of child advocates—social workers, philanthropists, teachers, administrators, all sorts of government workers, university professors and researchers, and the like—meant that a children's movement was in the making. By the end of the 1930s the movement could point to some solid achievements for children, but critics could also show that many of the ideas designed to improve society as a whole did so at the expense of the rights of children. Before these contradictions could be worked out, the nation was consumed by the Second World War.

Chapter Seven

Expanding Social Services for Children, 1940–1960

Not only did the Second World War transform global political realities but it also had a pronounced effect on American life. While the New Deal may have started the American economy on the road to recovery, most historians now agree that prosperity and full employment returned during the war itself. The recovering economy and the needs of the war had the largest effect on society. Families who had come together during the depression found their members spreading around the globe as the war went on.

As the demand for industrial production increased during the war, and young men who had registered for the draft were called up, industries had to offer new incentives to attract workers. Women began to work in defense plants early in the war, as they had done during the First World War, but World War II marked the first time that young mothers with small children did so as well. Although the desire for day care had been made abundantly clear during the 1930s, it was not until a wartime labor shortage developed that the government fully endorsed the idea of federally funded day care. The government provided some day-care assistance through the Lanham Act, and eventually some industries developed day-care centers.

Day care was a major issue largely because it challenged the American family ideal. Most Americans believed that mothers should remain home to take care of small children and that fathers alone should be breadwinners. Wartime necessity changed that pattern, and in spite of the efforts of many propagandists, women, including young mothers, have remained in the work force ever since.

The war and its aftermath raised a number of issues involving children, and those issues occupied the child advocates who would form the nucleus of the postwar children's rights movement. One dramatic issue was the question of juvenile delinquency. American authorities expected the dislocations of the war to lead to more youthful law-breaking, and accordingly, both the Justice Department and the Children's Bureau geared up to deal with the problem. Drawing their conclusions from the experience of the British early in the war, the two federal agencies argued over jurisdiction and prepared to meet a major challenge to American social peace. The propaganda factory that had been charged with getting women out of the work force so that there would be jobs for returning servicemen needed a scary issue to convince working mothers that their continued presence in the work force threatened their children. The propagandists and the federal agencies combined to put the specter of juvenile delinquency before the American public as a new menace to the future of the American dream.

Wartime Juvenile Delinquency

The delinquency rate did increase during the war, and that fact alone worried many adults. In 1946, for example, 42 percent of the respondents to one poll indicated that they believed that the current generation of young people behaved worse than their own generation had. At least one sociologist, Francis E. Merrill, believed that the increase in the delinquency rates had come from revised definitions of the meaning of delinquency and from a heightened public sensitivity to it.[1]

At the 1940 White House Conference on Children and Youth in a Democracy, the conferees worried about the problem of delinquency, and they acknowledged that the juvenile justice system did not make use of the latest findings in the study of child behavior. "Recent years," the final report concludes, "have brought considerable understanding of the reasons that make particular children delinquent and of ways of treatment that give promise of improvement in individual cases and may help to prevent delinquency in others." But, they added, "this recent knowledge has penetrated only in a meager way the procedures of many courts and institutions dealing with delinquent children."

The conference final report recommended a shift from treatment to prevention:

We know now a number of danger points or threats to child behavior that are conducive to delinquency. This is where prevention must begin. If it is true that the conditions of family life are the principal builders of conduct, then the breakdown or low level of family life is to be prevented, if possible. That means first a livelihood for the family, then normal surroundings, education of parents in the nature of child behavior, and psychiatric and social services available for helping people to deal with deep-seated problems of friction, unhappiness, and insecurity within the family.

The conferees also expected to identify predelinquent behavior in the schools and to combat it with special programs even before it began.[2]

Although delinquency increased during the war, the rate of increase was not very large. Nevertheless, the public's fears about juvenile crime were heightened because the predicted increase in delinquency had indeed occurred. The war had broken up families across the country, thus creating the very condition to which the 1940 White House conference had pointed.

Was juvenile crime up? It was hard to say because the reporting system for crime statistics was imprecise. Both the Federal Bureau of Investigation (FBI) and the Children's Bureau collected information about juvenile crime, and both agencies agreed that there had been an increase in juvenile crime during the war. After studying the evidence, however, historian James Gilbert concludes that the increase in juvenile crime early in the war "was probably not great enough to justify the attention focused on it during 1943 and 1944."[3]

The American public was aroused by sensational media attention to the issue of delinquency, especially a March of Time production, the late 1943 dramatic film *Youth in Crisis,* which included a speech by a director of the FBI, J. Edgar Hoover. The same year, Sen. Claude Pepper's Senate Subcommittee on Labor and Education began hearings on the educational and physical fitness of the American civilian population. The committee quickly found much of its time devoted to the perplexing issue of juvenile delinquency. The testimony indicated that at least part of the increase in delinquency could be traced to the behavior of "victory girls," young women who had sex with soldiers. The committee concluded, Janus-like, that juvenile delinquency was a serious problem, but that there was little evidence that it had increased during the war. The advice given to the Senate committee proved so contradictory that it recommended no action, and the problem of delinquency remained an active issue at the end of the war. In the 1950s there would be other even more sensational Senate hearings on juvenile delinquency, and the nation would continue to debate the issue.[4]

Society's concern over juvenile delinquency would eventually lead to a clearer codification of children's rights. But during the war and immediately after, the notion that young people had important legal rights separate from those of their family would have seemed foreign indeed. During the "zoot suit" riots of 1943 in Los Angeles, in which off-duty servicemen attacked young Hispanic-Americans wearing the outfits, most members of society agreed with the policy of arresting the teenagers. No one seems to have thought that they had the right to wear what they chose.

The zoot suit incident, the Senate hearings, and the sensational material coming from the FBI convinced the public, in spite of evidence to the contrary, that a serious youth crime wave was under way. The zoot suit incident indicated clearly that any youthful challenge to public authority during wartime was to be met with swift social sanctions. Thus, during the war children and youth may well have lost ground so far as their rights were concerned.

Most authorities agreed that the primary reason for the increase in delinquency was the breakup of the family, which had been caused by the dislocations of war and by too many mothers leaving home to work in defense plants. This charge and its emphasis on the plight of the "latchkey" children who remained unsupervised at home would be the persistent and principal content of the propaganda to convince women to leave the work force at the end of the war.[5]

Day Care During the War

The entrance of large numbers of young mothers into the work force during the war raised a number of social policy issues related to the question of children's rights. If the propagandists were right—that latchkey children were more likely to become delinquent—could it be argued that children had the right to have a parent at home? Similarly, could it be argued on behalf of younger children that mothers could not leave them and that day care was in one sense a violation of children's rights? Or could policymakers make a general appeal to children's rights as a way of arguing for the elimination of women, especially mothers, from the work force?

Nevertheless, the demands of industry could not be met with the work force in place in 1941, and it became necessary to attract a new pool of workers—mothers with small children. To deal with the problem of children thus being deprived of maternal care the Children's Bureau sponsored a conference in the summer of 1941. One of the goals of the conference was to coordinate the various federal day-care efforts sponsored by the WPA, the Office of Education of the Federal Security Agency, and the Children's Bureau.[6]

Two years later the situation had become a crisis. In response to an announcement from the War Manpower Commission, the author of an article in *Survey Midmonthly,* the nation's foremost journal of social work, observed that "the realization has dawned not only that many mothers *will* work but that in an increasing number of areas many mothers *must* work if the war production program is to proceed at full capacity. It is also being realized that day care must be provided for the children of these working mothers not only for the children's sake, but also in order to maintain top efficiency on the assembly line."[7] The interests of children, it seemed, were worth addressing if they had something to do with production quotas being in jeopardy.

Congress passed the Community Facilities Act, also known as the Lanham Act, in 1940 and subsequently amended it three times. In 1942 it was interpreted to allow support for day care. The procedures for receiving federal assistance for day care under the act were quite complicated, and no community received funds until late 1942. Other difficulties also hampered the use of federal funds for day care. Communities had to apply for the money and clear a series of bureaucratic hurdles. In addition, communities had to provide 50 percent of the operating funds of the centers. Many withdrew their applications on learning of this provision. On the positive side, however, many of the former WPA nursery schools were transferred to Lanham Act funding with relatively little difficulty.

During the great expansion of the work force during the war, adequate day care, like a great many other things, was in short supply. Lanham Act funds, while certainly helpful if they could be obtained, were by no means sufficient to meet the demand. Communities found other ways to provide child care, and industry frequently contributed to day-care programs.[8]

The peak of federally funded day-care centers came in July 1944 when there were 3,102 units in operation serving 129,357 children—a small percentage of those needing aid. While aiding the war effort was the primary justification for federal funding of day care, the Children's Bureau did make recommendations about the needs of the children themselves.

The bureau, mindful of children's developmental needs, recommended that infants under the age of two be cared for in a foster family setting rather than in group care. They also recommended that:

1. Decisions as to the care of young children should be made in the light of the child's needs, which should be given primary emphasis.

2. Every effort should be made to preserve for the young child his right to have care from his mother, since the normal development of the young child depends upon an affectional relationship with her.

3. Advisory and counseling service should be made available in every program of child care.

    ....

7. Public information should be developed on the needs of young children so that mothers may be better informed as to their importance to their children and better able to make sound choices in planning for their care.[9]

The Children's Bureau, an important player in the emergence of the mid-twentieth–century children's rights movement, was almost alone during World War II in seeing issues in terms of their effect upon children.

Child Health during the War

The health of American children, as measured by infant mortality rates, continued to improve during the 1930s and World War II. In 1928 the rate had been 69 per 1,000 live births. By 1938 the rate was 51 per 1,000. In the 1940s the nation finally came to understand and address pellagra, caused by malnutrition, and the problem of "blue babies." Better parent education may have also contributed to improved child health. Child-rearing advice during the war tended to stress loving care and individual attention—in sharp contrast to Americans' reactions to any youthful behavior perceived as a challenge to public authority.[10]

One significant development in the field of child health was the wartime Emergency Maternity and Infant Care Program (EMIC), which provided maternity care for the wives of enlisted men in the four lowest grades. According to an article in the American Medical Association *Journal,* "The need for medical care for these wives arose not only from their inability to pay for care but from the fact that they were nonresidents of the state or county, in most cases strangers in the towns where they lived and wholly uninformed as to medical resources." By the time the program ended in 1949 about 1½ million mothers and infants had received assistance. Although this program improved child health, Congress made it clear that EMIC's primary purpose was to improve the morale of American soldiers; the health of the child was a secondary concern. Children might claim the right to health, but the ways in which they received health care suggested that the country was not ready to honor such a claim on its own merits.[11]

The Children's Bureau started the EMIC program in Washington State on an experimental basis, using some of its own funds; it lobbied for and subsequently won approval for a comprehensive program. The bureau launched the program without the support of physicians, who objected to the idea on a number of grounds: "In the development of this program the physicians of the country were given no voice in the formation of plans and policies, although the carrying out of the program was of necessity dependent upon their efforts and cooperation. In other words the function and purpose of the Children's Bureau have been abruptly changed so that it is now an active factor in the practice of medicine throughout the United States, dictatorially regulating fees and conditions of practice on a federal basis." The American Academy of Pediatrics passed a resolution seeking a meeting between Children's Bureau officials, various physicians' organizations, the Public Health Service, and the American Hospital Association. The meeting was held, but the doctors were incensed that "a large group of individuals representing lay organizations such as the W.C.T.U., the Y.W.C.A., and the National Woman's Trade Union League," were also invited. They concluded that a medical meeting involving nonmedical representatives "defeated the purpose of the meeting."[12]

At least one pediatrician objected to the reactions of the organization. Grover F. Powers, professor of pediatrics at the Yale University School of Medicine, wrote in 1944 that "it seems a tragedy" that the action of the executive board of the American Academy of Pediatrics might give the public the idea that pediatricians were "more interested in preserving certain professional mores than in promoting the welfare of mothers and babies." The executive board had threatened to withdraw support from the Children's Bureau, and Powers objected strenuously to that idea. "Would it not be ungrateful, short-sighted, and unscientific, contrary to our own high purposes, and above all, against the best interests of America's children," he wrote, "to cease collaboration with our experienced

Children's Bureau friends[?]" These people he described as "tried and true crusaders in our common cause of maternal and child welfare."[13] The dispute with the pediatricians shows that the Children's Bureau was a principal advocate for the rights of children during the war, even when its efforts offended a group normally counted among its strongest supporters. Powers reminded his colleagues that they, too, could usually be counted among those who spoke out for children's interests.

Following the war, President Truman called for a program of national health insurance, an idea that was bitterly opposed by the American Medical Association. A bill to provide such insurance was introduced as early as 1945, but because of the opposition of the AMA, it never came to a vote. In 1946 Sen. Claude Pepper introduced a bill to provide maternal and child care, services to crippled children, and child welfare programs on a national basis. No action was taken on this bill, but the limited appropriations under the Social Security Act for these purposes were increased.[14] Only those children whose parents could qualify for state welfare assistance could expect some governmental support for their medical needs.

The Baby Boom

As the war ended, Americans hoped to enjoy the new prosperity of the country and to get on with their lives. They realized that some readjustments to peacetime living would be necessary, and they also understood that many wartime measures would come to an end. The New Deal and the war, however, had transformed American society—especially where the role of the federal government was concerned. Some federal programs—such as social security—were not controversial, but many others, especially those involving children, aroused strong public concern. Needless to say, few Americans wished to harm children or undermine their well-being; but the family ideal returned to center stage in postwar American life with particular force. Most child advocates have always been family advocates as well. But the very concept of children's rights implies that children have some legitimate claims even against their own families. An increase in the attention paid to the family ideal would imply a corresponding decline in interest in children's individual rights.[15]

In addition to great ideological emphasis on the family ideal, there seemed to be a concerted postwar effort on the part of young marrieds to recreate the large families of the nineteenth century. The birth rate soared, and this period became known as the years of the "baby boom."

The American birth rate and the continuing decline in the death rate combined to produce a tremendous population growth. In the 1930s demographers had predicted that the population of the United States would never exceed 200 million; by 1953 the population had already reached 160 million, and the birth rate was still increasing. What accounted for this expansion was what one student of the phenomenon has called the "procreation ethic," which resulted from a combination of factors: "the flush of military victory, the staggering prosperity, [and] the renewed faith in the future." The war and the depression had contributed to low fertility, but after the war it seemed possible for Americans to achieve their long-suppressed dream of creating large prosperous families.[16]

The postwar years, then, were a time for emphasizing traditional values, for reasserting the preeminence of family life, and for enjoying the fruits of victory and prosperity. Issues related to children, their rights, and their health receded. Most Americans seemed to think that things were going so well that social problems would take care of themselves. But the advocates for children's rights—the staff members at the Children's Bureau, the social workers who dealt with neglected, dependent, or abused children, the pediatricians who treated children suffering from all sorts of ills and abuse, the juvenile court judges and probation officers, members of civic clubs, and a host of other citizens—combined to focus on children's issues and problems even without the aid of national awareness or concern.

Day Care and Dependent Children after the War

Women still worked in great numbers after the war. Many wished to continue working in defense plants but found that the better jobs were being reserved for returning servicemen. So women had to take whatever employment they could find. The emphasis on the family ideal discouraged women from working outside the home but ignored the needs of many single women who had to support themselves. Day care, accepted because it had been a wartime expedient, now faded from public consciousness as an issue. But the need for day care had not faded; many women kept their jobs, and others entered the work force. For example, according to Margaret Steinfels, "between April, 1948 and March, 1966 the labor force participation of married women with husbands present and with children under six increased from 10.8 percent to 24.2 percent." These figures did not include widowed, divorced, or single mothers.[17]

These mothers usually had no choice but to make informal arrangements for the care of their children. The mothers themselves found these arrangements less than ideal, but the larger society, having embraced the family ideal, simply assumed that all mothers were staying home. In 1960 the Child Welfare League at last spoke out about the needs of the children themselves. Day care, it said, was a way "to protect children by providing part-time care, supervision and guidance when their families were unable to meet their needs without some assistance from the community." Three years later the Children's Bureau weighed in with the reminder that "day care makes it possible for many parents to keep their children with them in their own homes and to retain their legal and financial responsibility. Therefore, day care is a way of strengthening family life, preventing neglect of some children, and reducing risk of separation from their families for others."[18] While no one was contending that children have a right to day care, most people concerned about children's welfare agreed with the well-established right of children to a start in life, a start that includes both good health and a psychologically healthy environment. Like the Children's Bureau's articulation of policies for infant day care in World War II, this later statement of the bureau makes a case based on the needs of children themselves. The hope of child advocacy groups like the Child Welfare League and the Children's Bureau was that public policy could be based on children's needs (which some might label rights) rather than on expediency or unrealistic ideals.

Those who argued for expanded, publicly funded day care in the postwar years faced impossible odds. The forties and fifties were also the years of the "feminine mystique," as Betty Friedan labeled the pattern—the assumption that all mothers were following the ideal of staying at home—even though one-third of all American women worked outside their homes.[19] As if this were not enough, many experts in early child development believed that children could not thrive adequately in their early years without their mothers. Proponents of the "maternal deprivation syndrome" suggested that any mother who did not remain with her young child was doing that child permanent psychological damage. Later research has qualified the conclusions reached in the 1950s. Certainly infants need close contact with a parent, and they need constant attention, including physical care, touching and stimulation. Experts now agree that bonding with parents is important for infant development, but they disagree on whether bonding has to include continuous caregiving by the mother alone. The findings of developmental studies in the 1950s did show that institutional care for orphans and other dependent children was inadequate and harmful. These findings led to improved treatment of dependent children, but they also reinforced the family ideal. Attitudes about day care would not change until the 1960s when child-saving professionals began to articulate a stronger case for it.[20]

Public assistance to children whose parents lived in poverty was equally dismal during the immediate postwar period. Because the federal government required that all eligible candidates for ADC be treated equally, the number of children on the welfare rolls swelled dramatically and came to include both minority children and illegitimate children. As the welfare rolls increased after the war, however, taxpayers began to look with disfavor on the entire program. Many believed that dishonest and disreputable people were taking advantage of the largess of the new welfare system, and that welfare fraud was rampant. Politically motivated investigations into the system produced little solid evidence of fraud, but accounts in the press emphasized the cases of fraud that had been found and left the impression that the entire system was thus beset.

These public perceptions led to the passage, or attempted passage, in several states (mostly southern) of rules (aimed primarily at African-American women) that sought to limit or eliminate illegitimate births. The federal government resisted these efforts because the federal law creating ADC had made need rather than behavior the primary criterion for the granting of aid. But states adopted regulations that denied support to children whose mothers had either remarried or established a common-law relationship with another man. In effect, this rule required the live-in male friend or stepfather to be responsible for children not his own. It also denied support to a great many children who lived under these circumstances.

In the late 1950s eight southern states (Arkansas, Florida, Georgia, Louisiana, Mississippi, Tennessee, Texas, and Virginia) and Michigan adopted a new approach to deny welfare support to some families: they denied aid because of the "unsuitability" of the home of otherwise eligible children. This was an extremely ironic use of the concepts of child protection. Virtually all students of child abuse and neglect point to the poverty of the child's family as one of the major factors in the onset of abuse or neglect. Yet these southern states found a way to limit federal aid to their poorest citizens. The primary motivation seems to have been strong objections by the electorate to the granting of aid to minority children. In 1960 Louisiana announced that it was dropping approximately 6,000 families from its welfare rolls as a result of a "suitable home" law passed by the legislature in March of that year. So dramatic was this announcement and the press coverage it received that the outgoing secretary of health, education, and welfare, Arthur Fleming, announced a new federal policy that would eliminate the suitable home test. Southern states objected to the new policy, but Congress gave it the full force of law in 1961.

In the operations of ADC in the postwar years the nation was reneging on an old idea—that children, regardless of the behavior (or the race) of their parents, deserve an adequate start in life, and that the state has both parental power and parental responsibility under the doctrine of *parens patriae*. No one questioned the power of the state to take children from abusive parents, but the idea that this power carried with it a corresponding responsibility seems to have been lost on some Americans. Southern states had effectively disenfranchised their African-American citizens, and southern political leaders sought to also deny benefits to nonvoting citizens and keep taxes low in the process. Any notion that this action was in violation of the needs and long-recognized rights of children went unacknowledged.[21]

Postwar Delinquency

Meanwhile, the failure of the predicted epidemic of juvenile delinquency to materialize during World War II did not daunt the juvenile justice establishment in its efforts to command public attention and support. If the nation collectively turned its back on the needs of children whose mothers worked, it responded quickly to society's need to be protected from youthful behavior that challenged public authority. The continuing bureaucratic struggle between the FBI and the Children's Bureau was over how youthful misbehavior was to be understood—as lawbreaking or as the result of the special circumstances of young citizens. Ironically, if juvenile delinquency had been considered solely in the context of the adult criminal code, youthful offenders would have had more legal rights, especially procedural rights (see chapter 6). But public attention focused on some sensational Senate hearings and on the provocative testimony of one witness in particular.

The Senate Subcommittee to Investigate Juvenile Delinquency had been organized in 1953, but it became well known only after Sen. Estes Kefauver of Tennessee assumed the chairmanship in 1955. One reason for the notoriety of this committee was its attention to the role of the mass media in promoting juvenile delinquency. But because committee hearings were televised and attracted a large national audience (one survey indicated that at one time or another 86 percent of all the television

sets in the country had been tuned to the hearings),[22] they also contributed to the perception that delinquency was increasing rapidly and had
become a major social problem.

The list of witnesses before the Kefauver committee included experts
such as Katherine Lenroot of the Children's Bureau, Sheldon and Eleanor
Glueck, both well-known researchers in delinquency, Paul Lazarsfield,
an expert in communications theory, James Bennett, head of the federal
prison system; and Fredric Wertham, a respected psychiatrist and author
of *The Seduction of the Innocent,* a diatribe against comic books that recalled Anthony Comstock's famous *Traps for the Young.* Wertham was
the centerpiece of the process because he argued both that delinquency
was increasing and that comic books—especially crime comic books—
were causing it.[23]

Concern about comics and crime had been around before the hearings.
In August 1950 Kefauver had mailed a questionnaire to opinion leaders
throughout the nation asking if they knew of any links between comic
books and crime. The response was mixed. Wertham and a few others,
Bennett included, condemned the comics, but others, like Lenroot, defended them, leaving the senator without a clear verdict in this area.
Delinquency was a hot topic, however, and Sen. Kefauver continued to
work on it, moving for the creation of the special subcommittee in 1953
and becoming its chair in 1955.

The committee was underfunded, however, and borrowed a staff
member, Richard Clendenen, from the Children's Bureau. Clendenen
saw his role as one of both investigating the problem and "educat[ing]
the Senators to the fact that there are no easy answers for the problem
of juvenile delinquency," the position of the bureau. Clendenen had been
head of the privately funded Special Delinquency Project in the Children's
Bureau. The project culminated in a national conference in the nation's
capital in 1954. (Senators were not the only ones to bring experts to
Washington). The bureau's position at the conference was that improvements in the treatment of delinquency and research into its causes should
go forward simultaneously.[24]

Wertham appeared before the committee in early 1954 and repeated
his claim that crime comics caused juvenile delinquency. It also came out
at that point that some of the expert defenders of the crime comics had
served as paid consultants to the comic-book publishers. But the committee reached no firm conclusion about the relationship between juvenile
crime and comic books and thus recommended no new legislation.[25]

When Kefauver took over the committee, it began investigating the role of television in promoting juvenile crime, as well as the role of the movies, which had been self-regulated since 1934. Comic-book publishers had also developed their own code in order to escape official censorship. Kefauver appeared to have two goals in his hearings. On the one hand, he believed that self-regulation and local pressures would control the excesses of comics and the media; but on the other hand, he wished to respond to the strong public opinions about the excesses of comics and the media. The committee issued its final report in 1957; like most government reports, it recommended further study. In the debates between the experts who argued that the causes of delinquency were complex and those who believed that comic books should be banned, the experts had clearly won the day.[26]

What this victory meant was that the entire arena of juvenile justice was going to come under the control of members of the helping professions. Their research efforts and recommendations for changes in treatment would transform the entire system and effectively insulate it from public scrutiny. In the process, two threads would come together. From inside the system criticism of its workings had been accumulating since the 1920s; on the outside were social-science experts who wished to improve social knowledge about the causes of delinquency. The call of the Children's Bureau for simultaneous advances in theory and practice had been answered—at least insofar as more activity was concerned.[27]

As early as the 1920s some juvenile court judges worried about the broad powers their courts possessed and suggested that the court's functions be divided between regular courts and the schools. Some critics even went so far as to suggest that children be given some procedural protection when they appeared before juvenile courts. Not until the *Gault* decision by the U.S. Supreme Court in the 1960s (see chapter 8) did children gain these rights. Another concern was that children appearing before the court were being stigmatized by the label of "delinquent." The solution to this problem was to keep children out of court and to make the services of the court available informally. Most of these informal proceedings were handled by probation officers. Ironically, once a child became a part of the informal system, he or she was completely beyond the reach of the law. If a child appeared before a juvenile court judge, there was at least a chance that some sort of procedural rights would be respected.

In 1943, in response to the concern about labeling, the National Council on Crime and Delinquency, which published model juvenile court provisions, began deleting all references to the term *delinquency* in their draft. By 1959 about one-third of all states had adopted a nonlabeling approach. Still another response to the labeling issue was the creation of a new category, "persons [or minors] in need of supervision."[28]

For the nation as a whole, however, the issue seemed to be one of how best to respond to the rising challenge of juvenile crime. The Kefauver hearings, the reports from the Children's Bureau and the FBI, and the images of youth in films such as *Blackboard Jungle, Rebel without a Cause,* and *Blue Denim* suggested that the nation was about to be overcome by a wave of youth crime. By the early 1960s, however, the nation seemed to become aware that the emergence of a different and socially significant youth culture could no longer be ignored or misunderstood. According to historian James Gilbert, the real issue over juvenile delinquency in the postwar years was "in fact a misunderstanding or the expression of distaste for the development of youth culture."[29] Thus, a host of factors were involved in the public debate about juvenile delinquency. The actual rate of youthful misbehavior was only one small part of the debate; public misperception was the principal factor. Other players in the debate included social scientists, who expected to claim a larger public role by expanding the fund of knowledge about delinquency; federal agency staffers, whose concerns mirrored those of the social scientists and who also had a vested interest in maintaining juvenile delinquency as an important public issue; and those who staffed the nation's juvenile justice system. The latter group had already found one effective way to eliminate delinquency: rename it.

Conclusion

The two decades between the outbreak of the Second World War and the publication of Betty Friedan's *The Feminine Mystique* were among the most important in the twentieth century—and also among the most difficult to interpret. The exigencies of war caused major transformations in the social life of the nation as millions of men joined the armed forces and millions of women, including mothers of young children, entered the work force. These developments encouraged federal efforts to expand the social services available to families and children. Among the most prominent of these were the Lanham Act, which provided federal funds for day-care centers, and EMIC, which provided maternal and infant care to the wives and children of some enlisted men. These measures were justified in terms of wartime needs rather than on the basis of the needs or rights of children themselves, although the Children's Bureau did argue that standards for day care (and by extension, other programs) should be derived from the rights and needs of children.

For the most part, however, children and youth were the forgotten people during the war, and their efforts to create a meaningful role or style for themselves only aroused the condemnation of the nation as a whole. During and after the war the nation worried about the rise of juvenile crime and the role of comic books and the media in causing it. By the 1960s, however, the nation was beginning to see the emerging culture of youth in a more positive light. That new perspective would lead to an entirely different era in the history of children's rights, a time when a host of advocacy organizations sprang up to promote the rights and interests of American children.

After the war Americans tried vigorously to forget the sacrifices of war and depression, to emphasize family life, to live the good life, and to ignore the continued existence of social problems. Since according to the dominant ideology, women were supposed to remain at home, social policy, reflecting that ideology, ignored working women's need for day care. Because of the persistence of the family ideal in this period, children whose parents had not lived up to that ideal were punished for their parents' behavior, especially if they were members of a minority. The nation was in a period of denial so far as children's needs and rights were concerned.

But pressures to overcome this massive denial were mounting. Social scientists, perhaps more aware of realities than others, began to document the extent of social suffering in the United States, particularly children's suffering. Judges and probation officers within the juvenile justice system sought to improve it, and federal employees consistently sought to administer agency programs fairly and equitably without regard to race. Most important, however, was the growing civil rights movement. The milestones of that effort—the Supreme Court's *Brown* decision in 1954, the Civil Rights acts of 1957 and 1964, and most important of all, the Voting Rights Act of 1965—changed the political map of the South and began to end the radical discrimination of American society against its children of color.

Chapter Eight

The Children's Rights Movement Comes of Age, 1960–1990

In many respects, the children's rights movement is a creature of the last 30 years. Major developments of this period—the extension of procedural rights to young people in juvenile courts, greater public awareness of child abuse, and the passage of federal legislation requiring child protective agencies to try to support the family of a child rather than remove the child—cannot be fully understood without a knowledge of the history of the juvenile court and the history of child welfare policy and practices, as well as some understanding of how the complicated relationship between the state, the family, and the child has evolved.

The period since 1960 has seen not only the emergence of a full-fledged children's rights movement, with two separate (and almost antithetical) wings, but a vigorous public debate about the needs of American children. Major federal legislation affecting millions of children has been passed, and some traditional child advocacy groups have been reinvigorated, but at the same time there has also been a distinct turn away from the liberal agenda of the New Deal. It is difficult if not impossible to say whether or not American children are better off. Those whose families are poor, desperate, or homeless must pay a high price for the economic failures of their family, but millions of people who were outside the mainstream of American life at the beginning of this era now find that their children have access to the resources (but no guarantee of success from using them) that earlier generations of Americans used to obtain their success. In the same period the U.S. infant mortality rate *worsened* relative to that of other industrialized parts of the world. And parts of the United States (such as Memphis, Tennessee) have infant mortality rates comparable to those of Third World countries. Much of this problem can be traced to the poverty of some parts of our society, especially Appalachia and the Mississippi Delta. Thus, the most basic right of any child—the right to life itself—is dependent on the economic status of his or her parents, and that in turn varies by region and by race.

As Americans responded to the high drama of the civil rights movement—which was primarily an African-American struggle—some groups saw in the movement a way to make basic social change and thus gain freedom and self-respect for themselves. In 1964, in an effort to weaken and perhaps defeat the Civil Rights bill, Sen. Howard Smith of Virginia added an amendment prohibiting discrimination by sex as well as race. Intended to make the Civil Rights bill a laughingstock, Smith's effort backfired when Sen. Margaret Chase Smith of Maine threatened serious objections if the references to discrimination on the basis of sex were not kept. So the administration of President Lyndon Johnson, eager to pass a civil rights bill, moved to retain Smith's amendment, and it became a part of the law.[1]

In 1967 the U.S. Supreme Court handed down a path-breaking opinion in the arena of children's rights, *In re Gault,* which brought counsel and due process to the juvenile court. In the 1960s, as a part of Lyndon Johnson's Great Society, Congress created the Head Start program, which was designed to overcome the handicaps of poverty. But as the nation struggled with the war in Vietnam, and later with the issues of Watergate, social agendas faded for a time.[2] Yet from the standpoint of children's rights, the period since 1960 has been one of expansion and redefinition. Thirty years later, children seem to have more rights, and those rights have been spelled out in great detail. By 1990 there were also a host of groups claiming to speak on behalf of children; this increase in child advocacy has seemed to reinvigorate some of the older child advocacy groups, such as the American Humane Association. At present there are still many frustrations. It is one thing for society to agree that children are entitled to certain rights and treatments; it is another for all deserving children to be treated as if they had rights. Efforts to enforce the rights children are said to possess continue to be made.[3]

Even as the Civil Rights Act of 1964 was being passed, American women had begun to read and talk about a new and provocative book, Betty

Friedan's *The Feminine Mystique,* first published in 1963. Friedan looked at the gap between the expectations of young, middle-class married women in American society and the realities of their lives. As it turned out, many women felt isolated and trapped in their suburban homes. Friedan's book seemed to be the manifesto of a new effort on the part of American women to win freedom and dignity for themselves—a movement that would be similar to the civil rights movement, but that at first would clash sharply with the children's rights movement.[4]

Although the Civil Rights Act of 1964 included a section on discrimination on the basis of sex, women who complained to the Equal Employment Opportunity Commission (EEOC) received no assistance. This unresponsiveness of a federal agency to the concerns of women was due in part to their lack of a public pressure group, one like the National Association for the Advancement of Colored People (NAACP). To remedy this defect feminists founded the National Organization of Women (NOW) in 1966. Borrowing tactics and rhetoric from the civil rights movement, NOW began agitating for an end to discrimination on the basis of sex and for a national day-care policy.[5]

A few years later NOW would move away from their original agenda into full support for the Equal Rights Amendment (ERA) and other measures such as abortion reform, revision of the rape laws, and lesbian rights. In the process, NOW would become a women's liberation organization, and its members would challenge all the assumptions underlying the images of women and motherhood in American society. At this point in the development of the women's rights movement, the children's rights movement began to emerge. Women wanted the freedom to be fully themselves—to be free not to have children or to marry if they wished. At the same time child advocates began to insist that every child had the right to a full-time mother.[6]

The most vigorous defense of the rights of children in custody hearings came from three authors, Joseph Goldstein, Anna Freud, and Albert Solnit, whose *Beyond the Best Interests of the Child* had a major impact on child welfare policies and practices. They emphasized the importance of the "psychological parent" of the child, while psychoanalyst Selma Fraiberg argued the case for the child's right to consistent full-time mothering from his or her biological mother in *Every Child's Birthright: In Defense of Mothering.* As a result of these vigorous assertions of the child's claim to full-time mothering being made at a time when the women's rights movement was gearing up, feminists and child advocates found themselves in the 1970s in open antagonism.[7]

The Response to Child Abuse

Child protection workers began working on the issue of child abuse in the 1950s. In 1955 Vincent De Francis, a lawyer and head of the children's division of the American Humane Association, called a conference of child welfare professionals to discuss the problem of child abuse. Traditionalists argued against interference in family matters without invitation, but others argued for a more aggressive approach. The participation of a representative from the Children's Bureau in the conference may have led to the federal agency's increased activity in this area. Although professionals close to the problem felt a need for national action on the problem of child abuse, the public seemed unaware of the extent of child abuse and thus did not regard it as a national social problem. [8]

Only after the medical profession identified the "battered child syndrome" did the public awaken to the issue of child abuse. Doctors had certainly known of child abuse before it became a recognized finding, but because of social mores and the difficulty in confronting parents, medical personnel seldom reported it. The increasing use of X-rays, however, helped to provide irrefutable evidence of battered child syndrome. In 1946 a radiologist reported finding an association between subdural hematomas and factures of the long bones in children, a finding that suggested that severe beatings had occurred on several occasions. In 1961 C. Henry Kempe, a pediatrician at the University of Colorado School of Medicine, conducted a symposium for the American Academy of Pediatrics where he proposed the term "battered child syndrome" to describe the pattern of injuries he was seeing in his clinical practice. The following year the Children's Bureau held a symposium of its own on the problem of child abuse, and in that same year Kempe and several colleagues published an article on the syndrome in the *Journal of the American Medical Association*:

The battered child syndrome is a term used by us to characterize a clinical condition in young children who have received serious physical abuse, generally from a parent or foster parent. . . .

A marked discrepancy between clinical findings and historical data as supplied by the parents is a major diagnostic feature of the battered child syndrome. The fact that no new lesions, either of the soft tissue or of the bone occur while the child is in the hospital or in a protected environment lends added weight to the diagnosis and tends to exclude many diseases of the skeletal or hemopoietic systems in which lesions may occur spontaneously or after minor trauma. Subdural hematoma, with or without fracture of the skull, is, in our experience, an extremely frequent finding even in the absence of fractures of the long bones.[9]

They went on to urge not only that treatment be given the child but that cases be reported to the proper authorities so that legal proceedings could begin. They also warned against sending the child home for fear of further injury. Thus, child protectionists were joined by physicians in the campaign against child abuse, and on behalf of children against their abusive parents. The development of the battered child syndrome breached the wall protecting the family from outside intervention.

Experts made this dramatic change possible. Their presumed impartiality helped establish the view that scientific evidence could justify interference with the family and that the state would in fact invade the family to protect the lives and persons of the children. (The state has always had the legal authority to do so, but it frequently lacked public support.) Similarly, the definition of child abuse as a medical pathology aided other agencies in dealing with it. If child abuse is seen essentially as a sin or a crime, it is more difficult for authorities to act or obtain information.

As a result of the publicity surrounding the identification of battered child syndrome, and because of active lobbying by pediatricians, every state revised its laws on child abuse and required individuals to report cases of it. These new laws tried to overcome the reluctance of professionals to report cases by giving them immunity from lawsuits. States also encouraged the public to report cases of abuse and established 24-hour hot lines for such purposes. Child welfare workers were quickly overwhelmed with reports.[10]

Social scientists began studying rates of child abuse both to determine the extent of physical abuse in American society and to come to a consensus on national policy. A 1973 study, for example, found that there were relatively few large-scale variables that could be used to differentiate between abusing and nonabusing families, although a father's unemployment did seem to correlate with higher rates of child abuse. Other traits of abusing families included isolation and large size.[11] Another study—which also found that it was difficult to estimate the actual amount of child abuse actually taking place, in spite of the reporting laws—concluded that the primary factor in child abuse was the willingness of authority figures to use violence. The author concluded: "The basic question seems to be not which measure to select for combating child abuse but whether American society is indeed committed to the well being of all its children and to the eradication of all violence toward them, be it violence perpetrated by individual caretakers, or violence perpetrated collectively by society. If the answer to this question is an unambiguous yes, then the means and the knowledge are surely at hand to progress toward this objective."[12]

The national concern about child abuse reached Congress, where it found a powerful friend in the person of Sen. Walter Mondale of Minnesota. Even before Mondale took up the cause by holding hearings on child abuse, Cong. Mario Biaggi of Brooklyn, New York, had introduced a bill on child abuse but could not get it through the House Ways and Means Committee. Mondale's efforts led to the passage of the Child Abuse Prevention and Treatment Act of 1973. This law required states to meet federal standards on custody provisions, among which is one granting state child welfare agencies the power to remove a child from a family for three days if the agency believes the child is in danger.[13]

There was little articulate opposition to the federal legislation when it passed, but as the child welfare system absorbed it, critics emerged. One critic estimated that erroneous reports made up about 65 percent of all the communications regarding child abuse. "Besides being a massive violation of parental rights," he wrote, "the flood of unfounded reports is overwhelming the limited resources of child protection agencies, so that they are increasingly unable to protect children in real danger."[14] Robert Mnookin, a distinguished Stanford University law professor, criticized the regulations governing the entire child welfare system:

They are vague and open-ended, they require highly subjective determinations, and they permit intervention not only when the child has been demonstrably harmed or is physically endangered but also when parental habits or attitudes are adverse to the inculcation of proper moral values. Typical statutory provisions allow court intrusion to protect a child who is not receiving "proper parental care," "proper attention," "whose home is an unfit place for him [*sic*] by reason of neglect, cruelty, depravity, or physical abuse," or whose parents neglect to provide the "care necessary for his health, morals or well being."[15]

These vague standards were administered by a complex bureaucratic system involving social workers, social work administrators, probation departments, and judges of juvenile or family courts. It was common practice to remove children from their families and place them in foster homes. Most often removals were made "where the court determines the parents' supervision and guidance of the child are inadequate, where the mother is thought to be emotionally ill, or where the child has behavior problems." According to Mnookin, "Although highly publicized, cases involving child battery, where a parent has intentionally abused or injured a child are in a distinct minority."[16]

The number of children being removed over their parents' objections was increasing even before the passage of the federal legislation, and as Mnookin has indicated, they were being removed for reasons other than gross physical abuse. One objection to the removal process challenged its legal basis—the "best interests of the child" standard; another questioned the effect on the child of placement in a foster home.

Mnookin detailed a number of objections to the best interests standard. It ignored the interests of the parents, "making the process," as Mnookin said, "more high sounding but less honest." Mnookin also raised the question of how a judge would decide the best interest of the child. The judge would need information about parental behavior in the past and would then have to predict what they would do in the future. Then the judge would have to predict

the effect of removing the child from home, school friends, and familiar surroundings, as well as predicting the child's experience while in the foster care system. Such predictions involve estimates of the child's future relationship with the foster parents, the child's future contact with natural parents and siblings, the number of foster homes in which the child will have to be placed, the length of time spent in foster care, the potential for acquiring a stable home, and myriad other factors.[17]

When parental custody is at stake, the judge often has almost no information—not even information on where the child might be placed. Furthermore, Mnookin continued, even if the judge has an enormous fund of information, his or her ability to predict future behavior cannot be relied upon. Because of a lack of consensus in American society about such matters as moral values and child rearing, judges necessarily have relied on their own personal values in making their decisions. Thus, Mnookin concluded, "as long as the best interests standard or some equally broad standard is used, it seems inevitable that petitions will be filed and neglect cases will be decided without any clear articulation or consistent application of the behavioral or moral premises on which the decision is based." When class differences have been a factor, the biases of a judge have been even more open to question.[18]

Mnookin also raised the question of the effect of foster care on the children being placed. In that inquiry he was joined by a powerful set of authors: Joseph Goldstein, also a lawyer, Anna Freud, a psychoanalyst and daughter of Sigmund Freud, and Albert Solnit, a professor of pediatrics and psychiatry at Yale University. Their *Beyond the Best Interests of the Child* speaks directly to the issue of the impact of placement on the children themselves. Central to their argument is the concept of the "psychological parent" of the child. Psychological parenting—as distinguished from the accident of biology—is based "on day-to-day interaction, companionship, and shared experiences. The role can be fulfilled either by a biological parent or by an adoptive parent or by any other caring adult—but never by an absent, inactive adult, whatever his [or her] biological or legal relationship to the child may be."[19] The authors used this concept in criticizing the standard practice of child placement. Typically, the appropriate authorities—child welfare workers or the juvenile court acting on their recommendation—removed abused or neglected children and placed them in foster homes. Foster placement, an old idea even in colonial times, was intended as a way of protecting the child from the dangers of his or her family. Placement in a foster family was supposed to be a response to the right of the child to grow up in a safe or secure environment.

Goldstein, Freud, and Solnit found the foster home arrangement unsatisfactory. Children need a safe and emotionally consistent environment, but foster care is inherently temporary and subject to the bureaucratic whims of the court or the child welfare agency. As a result, foster parents do not invest sufficient emotional energy in the foster child and "find themselves deprived of the position on which parental tolerance, endurance, and devotion are commonly based, namely, that of being the undisputed sole possessor of the child and the supreme arbiter of his fate. What is left, apart from the conscientious fulfillment of a task once taken over, is the appeal made by a helpless immature being on the mature adult's concern."[20]

That appeal may be lacking or minimal to the older child, who is more likely to be troublesome. The temporary relationship thus created fails to promote the psychological parenting every child needs. Thus, the realities of foster care undermine the very purpose for which it is intended— to promote the best interests of the child. Accordingly, the authors recommended a new set of guidelines for child placement:

1. Placement decisions should safeguard the child's need for continuity of relationships.

2. Placement decisions should reflect the child's, not the adult's, sense of time.

3. Child placement decisions must take into account the law's incapacity to supervise interpersonal relationships and the limits of knowledge to make long-range predictions.

4. Placements should provide the least detrimental available alternative for safeguarding the child's growth and development.

5. The child in any contested placement should have full party status and the right to be represented by counsel.[21]

Goldstein, Freud, and Solnit supported their recommendations with a full discussion and abundant illustrative material drawn from actual cases. They proposed psychiatric treatment for abusing parents but oppose routine removal of abused children. They wished either to support and sustain the child's existing family or to remove the child quickly and permanently in cases of severe bodily injury.[22]

Beyond the Best Interests of the Child, coupled with the concerns of critics such as Mnookin, contributed to a major alteration in the workings of the nation's entire child welfare and juvenile court system. The federal legislation passed in 1973 also created the National Center on Child Abuse and Neglect, which was operated in conjunction with the child protection arm of the American Humane Association. The law was expanded in 1978 (P.L. 95–266) to include sexual abuse. By the end of the 1970s an expanded and highly sensitive child abuse reporting and responding system was in place.

Until the mid-1960s the principal mover in the effort to reduce or eliminate child abuse was the U.S. Children's Bureau, but by the end of the 1970s the National Center on Child Abuse and Neglect had largely supplanted the bureau. The center had begun to gather data about the relative incidence of child abuse in American society in the 1970s. From 1976 to 1982 the number of cases of child abuse, according to a 1984 report from the center, increased from 416,000 to 929,000. Professionals at the center admitted that the earlier reports had been based on data from only 23 states, while 36 states (not necessarily including all of the original 23) were represented in 1982. Although the data set was useless in measuring the rate of change in child abuse, it did provide important information about the kind of child abuse being reported in the United States in the late 1970s and early 1980s. Of the cases in the set, 64 percent involved some form of deprivation, 25 percent some form of physical injury, 17 percent emotional maltreatment, 6 percent sexual maltreatment, and 9 percent "other." These relative proportions did not change as more reports came in. The report also notes that the families of abused children tended to be younger than families with children of the same age in the general population.[23]

How did the system respond to abuse reports? The authors noted that "an undetermined proportion of maltreatment cases may not be reported, substantiated or receive protective services." As noted above, some of the reports may have been fraudulent. Consequently, it was difficult to tell how well society was responding to child abuse. Of those cases reported, nearly 80 percent of the maltreatment cases received some form of service, as did 70 percent of the sexual abuse cases; in all other categories the percentage receiving services exceeded 50 percent. The most common form of service was counseling, followed by support services, court action, and crisis services (in 11 percent of the cases). In 1976, 25.3 percent of the reported cases had resulted in the placement of children in foster homes. But by 1982, largely as a result of the Adoption Assistance and Child Welfare Act of 1980, which limited the use of foster care, the percentage was down to 13.4 percent.[24]

Thus, the problem of child abuse had aroused national concern, which led to the passage of laws on both the state and national levels that encouraged the reporting and treatment of child abuse. The influence of a major work, *Beyond the Best Interests of the Child,* changed the way Americans dealt with the problem of child abuse. More cases were reported, more services were provided, and fewer children were taken from their homes. Those children who were removed undoubtedly came from situations where serious physical abuse had occurred. But most reported cases involved neglect rather than physical abuse, and the system had to be forced to adjust to that reality. The efforts of experts combined with a strong public concern to change the system. Along the way, children's right to be free from abuse was acknowledged, but in a way that tried to preserve parental rights as well. Just as the system for dealing with child abuse was modified in the 1970s, so too was one part of that system—the juvenile court.

The Transformation of the Juvenile Court

No case from juvenile court reached the Supreme Court until 1966. In *Kent* v. *United States,* the Court considered the nature of proceedings in juvenile court and found them seriously deficient. Morris A. Kent, aged 16, had been arrested for robbery and rape and detained in the Receiving

Home for Children in Washington, D.C., without a hearing. Kent's mother retained a lawyer, who sought a hearing on the question of whether or not the juvenile court would waive its jurisdiction and transfer the case to criminal court. In addition, the lawyer sought access to the social service case file on Kent, as well as psychological and psychiatric examinations for the teenager. The Supreme Court found that

the Juvenile Court judge did not rule on these motions. He held no hearing. He did not confer with petitioner or petitioner's parents or petitioner's counsel. He entered an order reciting that after "full investigation, I do hereby waive" jurisdiction of petitioner and directing that he be "held for trial for [the alleged] offenses under the regular procedure of the U.S. District Court for the District of Columbia." He made no findings. He did not recite any reason for the waiver. He made no reference to the motions filed by petitioner's counsel. We must assume that he denied, *sub silento,* the motions for a hearing, the recommendation for hospitalization for psychiatric observation, the request for access to the Social Service file, and the offer to prove that petitioner was a fit subject of rehabilitation under the Juvenile Court's jurisdiction.

The Supreme Court concluded that Kent was entitled to a hearing, "considering particularly," in the words of Justice Abe Fortas, "that decision as to waiver and transfer of the matter to the District Court was potentially important to petitioner as the difference between five years' confinement and a death sentence." Had Kent gone first to the District Court, there the motions of his counsel would have required a response on the record. He would have had more procedural rights in the adult criminal courts than in the court that was supposed to be acting on his behalf.[25] Although *Kent* required only that a hearing be held, the case was significant for being the Supreme Court's first close look at the peculiar nature of the juvenile court.

The complete lack of procedural rights and the absolute authority of the judge in juvenile court proceedings troubled many observers of the court in the early 1960s. New York, for example, had already begun the practice of having children represented by counsel in the juvenile court (after 1962 in New York, called the family court). In 1960 the Legal Aid Society began a pilot program to determine the impact of children being represented by lawyers, a project initiated by the New York Citizens' Committee for Children working with the New York City Bar Association. The attorneys for the project, headed by Charles Schinitsky of Legal Aid, were members of the Young Lawyers Division of the American Bar Association (ABA). The lawyers found numerous instances of fundamental unfairness. According to a study of the project, "The nature of the hearings and the purpose of the judgments were rarely explained to the children, who sometimes realized the seriousness of their situation only when they were placed in detention, and who had no way of knowing whether the testimony offered against them was legal." The project led to the Family Court Act of 1962, which also provided for legal representation through the Legal Aid Society for children who lacked an attorney of their own.[26]

Procedurally, at least, the courts in New York City were substantially ahead of the courts in the District of Columbia, although both suffered from politically appointed judges. At about the same time California overhauled its juvenile justice system—as the result of changes within the system, however, not bcause of public pressure.[27]

To understand the transformation of the juvenile court, it is necessary to look closely at the changes brought to the court and the juvenile justice system by the path-breaking case of *In re Gault* in 1967. The facts of the case were simple. A 15-year-old boy, Gerald Gault, was caught making obscene phone calls. Following a hearing before a juvenile court judge in Arizona, Gault was sent to the state industrial school until he reached the age of 21. His parents sued, claiming that their son's procedural rights had been violated. The Arizona Supreme Court turned down a petition for Gault's release, but in *In re Gault* the Supreme Court disagreed and laid down new principles for due process in juvenile courts. Justice Abe Fortas in the majority opinion noted that

the essential difference between Gerald's Case and a normal criminal case is that safeguards available to adults were discarded in Gerald's Case. The summary procedure as well as the long commitment was possible because Gerald was 15 years of age instead of over 18.

If Gerald had been over 18, he would not have been subject to Juvenile Court proceedings. For the particular offense immediately involved, the maximum punishment would have been a fine of $5 to $50, or imprisonment in jail for not more than two months. If he had been over 18 and had committed an offense to which such a sentence might apply, he would have been entitled to substantial rights under the Constitution of the United States as well as under Arizona's laws and constitution.[28]

In concurring, Justice Hugo Black made the view of the Court crystal clear: "Where a person, infant or adult, can be seized by the State, charged, and convicted for violating a state criminal law, and then ordered by the State to be confined for six years, I think the Constitution requires that he be tried in accordance with the guarantees of all the provisions of the Bill of Rights made applicable to the States by the Fourteenth Amendment."[29] The opinion set a higher standard of due process for juvenile court proceedings and in some respects extended the reforms of New York's Family Court Act of 1962 to the nation as a whole. In the process, the Court also found the concept of *parens patriae* to be "murky."[30]

Rather than fight to reestablish the basis for separate jurisdiction for juvenile offenders and to reclaim the juvenile court's unchecked authority, the system found a way to stay clear of the court almost completely. The diversion of young people from the courts was part of a larger effort that one scholar has labeled "decarceration." Both liberals and conservatives wished to limit the juvenile court, but for different reasons. Conservatives wanted to "get tough" on juvenile crime and therefore sought to limit the jurisdiction of the relatively "soft" juvenile court; liberals, on the other hand, wished to broaden the civil liberties of the children who appeared before it. These two positions coalesced into the notion that children and society are better served if young people are not a formal part of the juvenile justice system. While this objective was consistent with the original purposes of the juvenile court, the effect was to increase the number of young people who are in the system but have not officially been processed by it.

Because of strong objections of such child advocates as social workers and lawyers to status offenses, and also because of the *Gault* decision, most states revised their juvenile justice statutes to eliminate references to noncriminal offenders, who became "persons in need of supervision" (PINS) or an equivalent. (In some states, Tennessee, for example, children in this category are denied the procedural rights that *Gault* requires, although the procedural rights granted to juveniles accused of crimes exceed what *Gault* requires.)[31] This approach has reformed the juvenile court but left the system intact. According to sociologist John R. Sutton, the primary purpose of reform efforts was "to seal off the system from criticism and to preserve a domain of discretionary action in which the routine work of classifying and sanctioning delinquents is legitimated by substantive claims of professional expertise."[32]

In spite of the growth of the administrative side of juvenile justice— that part of the system that is not answerable directly to the court— *Gault* and reforms like those in California and New York made the juvenile court more concerned about due process. As one recent study of the workings of the juvenile court observes: "Once children were locked away and forgotten. Due process, now that it is being applied to children, makes such forgetting difficult: it forces those in authority to take a look, from time to time, at the children who have been placed in institutions. Due process suggests that if a child must be punished, that punishment must be combined with some degree of concern that the child not go on being punished for a lifetime."[33] This attention to due process is a major advance in the rights of children; it was brought about by litigation (by Gault's parents, among others) and legislation (New York's Family Court Act of 1962), by internal reform within the system (California) and by pressure from citizen organizations (the New York Citizens' Committee for Children). These disparate groups and individuals may not have known each other or even have known of each other, but together they may be called a movement. By the end of the 1970s they had broadened the scope of children's rights—to include the right to due process—in one important arena, the juvenile court.

Litigation and Children's Rights

Gaining due process rights for children would have been unthinkable without the active and effective participation of lawyers. Public-interest lawyers like Charles Schinitsky brought formidable skills to bear on some of the problems of the juvenile justice system. After they began their reform work, they found that the system required their continual presence to ensure its proper operation. "The bottom line," Schinitsky is reported to have said, "is basic fairness."[34] The system held (and holds) no shortage of challenges to fairness and no limit to the need for strong legal advocacy on behalf of children.

In granting children the right to have counsel before the juvenile court, the *Gault* decision required that lawyers begin to learn about the peculiar workings of the American child welfare and juvenile justice system. "System" may be too fine a label for the interlocking processes of the bureaucracies that deal with children in trouble. According to John R. Sutton, "Overall, local juvenile justice systems have become more complex; they have developed patronage links with sponsors at progressively higher levels of government; and they have become more similar, at least in terms of formal structure."[35]

Even though the system has become more complex, it really does not work very well. It has not reduced juvenile or adult crime, and it certainly has not had much of an impact on the rate of child abuse or neglect. Still, some internal changes have made the system more responsive to chil-

dren's needs, and it has been forced (while resisting vigorously) to respect both fairness and the rights of the children who come into it.

The principal means by which these changes have been and are being
made is through litigation and other legal measures. The professionals
who have brought the most sweeping changes to the child welfare and
juvenile justice system in the United States and can claim to be the most
effective element in the children's rights movement are the lawyers.
They have worked primarily in two ways: filing suits against recalcitrant
systems and agencies, and representing clients within the system as
guardians *ad litem* or as court-appointed special advocates (CASAs).
Both reform methods have worked, but the inertia of the system remains
strong.

Perhaps the best example of successful litigation on behalf of children
is *Pennsylvania Association for Retarded Children (PARC)* v. *Commonwealth of Pennsylvania,* a case filed in 1972. PARC was a special-interest
group organized to protest against the Pennsylvania practice excluding
many mentally handicapped children from the public schools. The case
was settled by a consent decree, so strong was the argument brought
by PARC. The federal district court that heard the case agreed that excluding mentally retarded children from the schools was unconstitutional.
The court held that the state could not deny retarded children an education without holding a hearing, and that by providing public education
to some children but denying it to others, Pennsylvania may have been
in violation of the equal protection clause of the Fourteenth Amendment.
One result of this case, combined with a ground swell of support for such
children, was the passage in 1975 of the Education for All Handicapped
Children Act (P.L. 94–142).[36]

The purpose of the law was to assure to all handicapped children "a
free appropriate public education which emphasizes special education and
related services designed to meet their unique needs, to assure that the
rights of handicapped children and their parents or guardians are protected, to assist States and localities to provide further education for all
handicapped children, and to assess and assure the effectiveness of efforts to educate handicapped children."[37] It is interesting that one of the
purposes of the law was to ensure the rights of handicapped children and
their parents or guardians. Agitation, litigation, and legislation appear to
be the necessary antecedents to the exercise of some of the rights children may claim.

Still, some critics worry that litigation alone may not be sufficient. In
1985 Robert Mnookin and others studied five difficult cases to try to

answer the question, "Is test-case litigation a sensible way to promote the welfare of children?" The authors could provide no definitive answer to the question but did illuminate some of the difficulties involved, such as how to determine the best interests of children. In the celebrated *Brown* case of 1954, for example, Mnookin notes that "the civil rights movement used a children's case—not a voting case or a case involving housing—to dismantle segregation. How many children were unconsenting foot soldiers sent off to war by judges and parents fighting to save this nation's soul? Subsequent generations owe them a great deal."[38] In a review of Mnookin's book, Gary Melton, a psychologist, points out some of the difficulties of pursuing a strategy of litigation: "Children's litigation almost inevitably requires the cooperation of government agencies, because children—especially the most vulnerable children—often are under the direct control of public schools, social service agencies, or juvenile courts. . . . Administrative discretion is hard to monitor and difficult to argue, and courts have few practical remedies available for recalcitrance by state officials."[39] These difficulties have not prevented the continued use of litigation as a weapon in the fight for children's rights. For example, the American Civil Liberties Union (ACLU), through its Children's Rights Project, "a national program of litigation, advocacy and education," is working "to ensure that when government child welfare systems must intervene in the lives of children, they do so according to Constitutional and statutory standards of fairness and due process, and in accordance with reasonable professional standards. The Project seeks to ensure that child welfare systems provide appropriate services and treatment for children and families as required by law."[40] This project is a continuation of the trend begun—if the *Brown* case is to be counted— in the 1950s. Only in the last few years, however, have lawyers turned specifically to the area of child welfare impact litigation, a new arena without legal precedents. According to one recent study, "The closest legal analogy that can be drawn is to the situations of mental patients challenging conditions in mental hospitals, and prisoners challenging conditions in penal institutions."[41] In 1981 and 1982, in the cases of *Lassiter* v. *Department of Social Services* and *Santosky* v. *Kramer,* the Supreme Court decided in the former case that indigent parents about to be faced with the loss of a child or children were not entitled to have a lawyer appointed for them, and in the latter case that in proceedings where parental rights are about to be severed, the standard of proof would have to be "clear and convincing" rather than "a preponderance of the evidence."[42] In a 1981 case in Kentucky the District Court found that "all parties to the child welfare system—parent, child, and foster parent—have a right to adequate administrative reviews when services of any sort are denied, terminated or modified."[43] Whether continued due process litigation might prove beneficial remains uncertain, but a recent study observed that "child welfare systems are plagued with arbitrary and largely unreviewed decision making. The possibility of being held to account, being forced to justify actions, usually has at least some impact on decision making." This process works "when and if there are individuals who will assert their right to these due process procedures."[44]

Another approach to take in such litigation is to sue for damages. Failure to follow procedures (such as obtaining a court order before placing children in a foster home) and failing to supervise foster homes has led to damage awards being sustained against child welfare agencies. This approach, however, fails to address the system as a whole; winning such cases serves only the interests of the individuals involved.

Yet another approach in litigation has been to take on an entire system. Early cases failed because plaintiffs could not find a constitutionally mandated remedy. The enactment of the Adoption Assistance and Child Welfare Act of 1980 helped to clarify the issues raised over the performance of child welfare systems when they removed children from their biological families. A case filed in Kentucky even before passage of the federal law resulted in another consent decree in which all parties agreed that children should be placed permanently as soon as possible once such a course had been determined, and that the procedures followed would be monitored.[45]

Another noteworthy case, brought by the Massachusetts Committee for Children and Youth, *Doe* v. *Matava,* was filed in state court on behalf of neglected and abused children. The case was settled in 1984 when agreement was reached between the plaintiffs and the state welfare agency that they would work together to improve the operation of the Massachusetts system. A similar case in New Mexico, *Joseph A.* v. *New Mexico Department of Human Services,* filed in 1981, cited the Adoption Assistance and Child Welfare Act as the basis for the suit. In denying a motion for partial summary judgment, the District Court noted that the plaintiff had submitted evidence "tending to show that the defendants acted with utter disregard for the controlling statutes and regulations." In other words, the suit had been filed to force the bureaucrats to follow the law with regard to children under their control.[46]

These and other cases have established some basic premises about children's rights *within* the child welfare system, including:

1. The right [of children] to sue government agencies and to appear in court through "self-nominated next friends who have no formal legal connection to them." (Thus, citizens' groups can sue on behalf of children in the welfare system.)

2. Issues involving children and child welare have become federal issues; they are not exceptions, as are most cases involving "domestic relations."

3. Children can sue government agencies to challenge the quality and appropriateness of treatment.

4. In combination with the Adoption Assistance and Child Welfare Act, state regulations "may create constitutionally protected property interests. In the case of statutes relating to access to adoption, and preventive services to avoid the need for foster care placements or to facilitate return to biological parents, these laws may also create constitutionally protected liberty interests."[47]

In sum, impact legislation has broadened some of the legal rights of children under the control of the state. The state may be the ultimate parent of the child (although the *Gault* case raised doubts about *parens patriae*), but even the state must treat such children fairly.

Upon reflection, however, the role of lawyers in bringing such cases is somewhat different from the role they take in most litigation. "Lawyers," one recent study notes, "are not, after all, social planners." Yet effective legal practice in cases involving state welfare agencies may not bring about the best results for the children in whose interest a suit is brought. Typically, such cases have resulted in considerable negotiation, partly because the conditions present in the welfare system before the suit was filed remained in effect. Thus, the role of the attorney—even as litigation has helped to create additional ways for children to make claims against the child welfare system—has also changed from that of vigorous advocate to that of conciliator.[48]

Special Advocates for Children

Closely related to the process of filing impact litigation is the process of representing children and their interests. Again, the key case is *In re Gault*, which required the juvenile court to respect due process. In addition, the development of guardians *ad litem* and CASAs enabled children to be represented by attorneys or special advocates in court proceedings. After *Gault,* these court-appointed advocates (the distinction between guardians *ad litem* and CASAs has since blurred) began to appear in all kinds of cases—not just those involving delinquency—and particularly in protective and custody hearings. A special pilot project for CASAs was begun in Seattle in 1977 using lay volunteers, an idea supported by the National Council of Juvenile Court Judges. As of 1987 there were 60 such programs around the country. Sometimes the CASAs would work closely with attorneys, sometimes not.

According to at least one study, lay volunteers performed as effectively as lawyers, although the volunteers in this study had legal training.[49] The authors of this 1987 study also point out that most lawyers lacked training in the representation of children, although the Young Lawyers Division of the American Bar Association had begun a special project in this area in 1985 and the *Children's Legal Rights Journal* had begun publication in 1979. In addition, children had been represented by attorneys in New York courts since 1962. Nevertheless, legal representation for children, particularly in nondelinquency cases (mostly involving abuse and neglect), expanded dramatically in the 1980s. Since 1985 the ABA's Young Lawyers Division has published the *Child Advocacy and Protection Newsletter,* which contains news of recent helpful publications and notices of special programs in various states—for example, the "In re kids" program in Utah—to inform lawyers of issues and developments in the area of child protection. In the January 1989 issue the editors described a study undertaken by the Massachusetts Bar Association to determine the unmet legal needs of children. Among other findings the Massachusetts study recommended:

1. clearer standards for intervening in families;
2. the appointment of counsel in cases where parental rights were to be terminated;
3. standards for termination;
4. a special children's service division within the program that provided public defenders;
5. a statute defining the role of the guardian *ad litem*; and
6. providing counsel for children in custody cases.[50]

Thus, lawyers have had a major impact on the expansion and clarification of children's rights and, whether they realize it or not, should be numbered among the most effective of the foot soldiers of the children's rights movement.

The Child Liberationists

As lawyers were pressing courts to provide remedies for children caught in the snares of the child welfare system, and as they worked for justice for their clients in the juvenile courts of the nation, others were also becoming vocal on behalf of American children. These new advocates seemed more radical and more strident than anyone seen before and fell into two broad groups: the child liberationists, who would grant children virtually the same rights adults possess and who would therefore in many respects blur the distinctions between adult and child; and the child protectors, who bring vigorous public lobbying to bear on issues of importance to children.[51]

Probably the most outspoken and forthright child liberationist is Richard Farson. His work *Birthrights* (1974) eloquently states that the best way to create a better, safer world for children is to endow them with a full slate of rights. Farson believes that "our world is not a good place for children . . . [because] every institution in our society discriminates against them. . . . Our society refuses to recognize their right to full humanity." But Farson believes that this view of children might change:

The civil rights movement and the various liberation efforts which it has ignited have alerted us to the many forms oppression takes in our society. As a result, we are now seeing the children as we have not seen them before—powerless, dominated, ignored, invisible. And we are beginning to see the necessity for children's liberation. . . . In the developing consciousness of a civilization which has for four hundred years gradually excluded children from the world of adults there is the dawning recognition that children must have the right to full participation in society, that they must be valued for themselves, not just as potential adults.

Farson thinks that modern society has actually compressed the rights that children possess. By granting rights to children, Farson believes that their lost childhoods might be restored. "Children are now so dominated and programmed," he concludes, "that they are indeed being robbed of childhood."[52]

John Holt has been another strong advocate for child liberation; his *Escape from Childhood* (1974) makes a case similar to that in *Birthrights*. "I have come to feel," Holt writes, "that the fact of being a 'child,' of being wholly subservient and dependent, of being seen by older people as a mixture of expensive nuisance, slave, and super pet, does most young people more harm than good."[53]

Both Farson and Holt propose granting "adult" rights to children. Holt would grant to children:

1. The right to equal treatment at the hands of the law—i.e., the right, in any situation, to be treated no worse than an adult would be.

2. The right to vote, and take full part in political affairs.

3. The right to be legally responsible for one's life and acts.

4. The right to work, for money.

5. The right to privacy.

6. The right to financial independence and responsibility—i.e., the right to own, buy, and sell property, to borrow money, establish credit, sign contracts, etc.

7. The right to direct and manage one's own education.

8. The right to travel, to live away from home, to choose or make one's own home.

9. The right to receive from the state whatever minimum income it may guarantee to adult citizens.

10. The right to make and enter into, on a basis of mutual consent, quasi-familial relationships outside one's immediate family—i.e., the right to seek and choose guardians other than one's own parents and to be legally dependent on them.

11. The right to do, in general, what any adult may legally do.[54]

Holt's list of proposed rights and Farson's views are typical of the child liberationists. They believe that the problems American children face stem from fundamental principles—such as the "family ideal" described by historian Elizabeth Pleck—and therefore propose a radical change in the way society relates to children. "The new child advocates," writes Howard Cohen, "see the standard, normal, socially acceptable treatment of children as part of the problem. It is the very institution of American childhood which they are attacking." The liberationists regard American childhood as the "systematic mistreatment of children." Part of the problem, the liberationists have argued, stems from some of the ways Americans have dealt with the mistreatment of children in the past. For the most part those efforts could be labeled "child protection" or "child saving."[55]

According to Farson, "The greatest resistance to the prospect of children's liberation will predictably come from those who are closest to the problem: parents, teachers, and children themselves." Both Farson and Cohen acknowledge that the child protectionists strongly oppose the liberationists. After all, the protectionists have felt that the best way to guarantee children's safety is to control them almost totally. Cohen challenges some of the assumptions made by the protectionists—such as the idea that "adults are able to perceive what is in a child's best interest." He disagrees with the notion that there is no conflict of interest between a well-meaning adult and a child, and he also questions the notion "that the quality of care can be improved by passing control over children from adult to adult."[56]

Reacting in a similar way to the situation of American children is Neal Postman, who laments the disappearance of American childhood. Postman cites as evidence the decline in the numbers of real children on television shows; in his view, most children on television behave like miniature adults. Similarly, he believes that adults are depicted as children, especially on the game show, "which is a parody of sorts of a classroom in which childlike contestants are duly rewarded for obedience and precociousness but are otherwise subjected to all the indignities that are traditionally the schoolchild's burden." Postman also cites the entry of children into professional and world-class amateur sports as an example of the disappearance of childhood and points to the distressing increase in crime committed by youth under the age of 15. "If America can be said to be drowning in a tidal wave of crime," Postman observes, "then the wave has mostly been generated by our children."[57]

Postman believes that much of this social pathology, while not created by the liberationists, rests on the same philosophy they espouse. Of Farson and Holt he writes, "Such a child's rights movement as this may be said to be a case of claiming that the disease is the cure." Or, as he also puts it more neutrally, the children's liberation movement is "an attempt to provide a rationalization for what appears to be an irreversible cultural tendency. Farson, in other words, is not the enemy of childhood. American culture is."[58]

The Child Protectors

Other child advocates have pushed various agendas designed to improve conditions for children in society as a whole, in the schools, in families, in the juvenile justice system, or in combinations of these contexts. For the most part these advocates—the protectionists, or the "carektakers," as Cohen calls them—do not object to the idea of rights for children, but they are less willing to grant full autonomy or adulthood to young people. They define children's rights in terms of claims on the larger society, while the liberationists believe that only the granting of complete legal freedom will enable children to protect themselves. Several issues have arisen from this debate, but the disagreement about the relative abilities of children and youth is only one minor difference between the protectors and the liberationists. They differ most vigorously on the issue of the role of adults in improving conditions for children in our society. Even Farson is willing to concede some role for adults in the articulation of children's needs and interests, but he expects that role to decline eventually. By contrast, many of the adults who work most closely with children think that they and others like them should have a continuing voice in the effort to win better treatment for American children.[59]

In *No One Will Lissen,* Lois G. Forer has provided an example of advocacy for one part of the American child welfare system. Forer served as an attorney for juveniles who appeared before the juvenile court in Philadelphia in the 1960s. "None of them," she writes, "expected that innocence would result in acquittal in a court of law, or that the law would provide redress for the wrongs they had suffered." Forer hoped that by writing an exposé of the system some reform would result, but she notes that the system seems to have its own logic. "At one point," she writes of her time as an attorney, "the juvenile correctional authorities complained that they did not have enough inmates to operate the institutions. It takes a lot of children to wash the dishes, scrub the floors, serve the meals, and care for the grounds of the institution."[60]

Those who work directly with children have frequently become their advocates. Early childhood specialists, for example, have a continuing tradition of being active on behalf of their young clients. Their professional organization, the National Association for the Education of Young Children, recently issued a book, *Speaking out: Early Childhood Advocacy,* which outlines the process of child advocacy. "Children need us to vote, to lobby, to inform and to speak out on their behalf. As early childhood educators, in partnership with parents and other concerned adults, we have the power to create change." Interspersed throughout the work are examples of advocacy in action—improving public understanding of early childhood education, building community awareness of the number of war toys for sale, holding a conference on the need for child care, and standing up for adequate salaries for child-care workers.[61]

Similarly, in 1984 the flagship journal for psychologists in the United States, *American Psychologist,* carried an article entitled "How to Influence Social Policy Affecting Children and Families." The article recites familiar and depressing data on the rise in the number of children living in poverty and in the number of homeless families. The article cites as a victory the effective lobbying of the American Psychological Association (APA) to prevent cuts in the funding of social science and psychological research. The authors also point to some notable failures in child and family-oriented legislation. "Concern about child and family policy in this nation," they write, "peaked in about 1971 when the Child Development Bill [Comprehensive Child Care Act] passed both houses of Congress." The time seemed right for such a bill, but "just when the bill seemed assured passage with bipartisan support, Congress was deluged with sacks of opposing mail all repeating almost verbatim, charges that the bill would lead to the 'sovietization of American youth' and a communal approach to child rearing." The authors believe that the New Right organized the pressure that led President Nixon to veto the bill, and as a result, "support for child and family policy went downhill for the next 10 years." They also explained that, at the same time, the coalition of children's advocates (never very well coordinated) seemed to come completely apart. "Congress noted that child advocates, already formed in the loosest of coalitions, were not even able to agree among themselves and so saw little payoff in support of [children's] legislation." More serious than the defeat of this one bill was the fact that "children's issues lost their Congressional forums." They propose rebuilding the coalition in support of children's issues and broadening its base. They also suggest that the Multigenerational Coalition on Dependent Care might achieve bipartisan support for programs for children and the elderly, and they approve the emergence of a specialized interest group, "Kids Pac," which contributes to the campaigns of candidates committed to working for children and families. They lament the failure of the 1980 White House Conference on Children and the apparent demise of this historically important series. The authors call on APA members to work for the reinstatement of the 1990 Conference on Children and to recognize the need to work to influence social policy.[62]

While many organizations and associations working with children have become active on behalf of children's interests (and their own when they coincide), the increased awareness of children's rights has also had an impact on the professionals who work with children. Judith Mearig has made a noteworthy examination of this process; she lists six areas where the children's rights movement "has influenced the professional's ethical responsibility":

1. The children's rights movement has challenged us to examine the origins of our beliefs concerning a child's best interests.

2. The children's rights movement has revealed the complexity of protecting children in our routine procedures.

3. The children's rights movement has helped to expose the autocratic use of individual professionals' power and judgment.

4. The children's rights movement has stimulated professionals to reconsider ways of responding to parents.

5. The children's rights movement has heightened professions' concerns with gaps in services, discrepancies between the way children should be served and the way in which they are actually served, and the policy implications.

6. The children's rights movement has underlined the necessity for individual professionals to go beyond traditional ethical guidelines and to take personal risks to serve children's best interests. [63]

Thus, just when professionals have joined the children's rights movement, they have had to acknowledge the impact of the movement on their own ideas and practices.

The best-known and arguably the most important of the children's advocacy groups has undoubtedly been the Children's Defense Fund (CDF) of Washington, D.C. It is headed by two important women: Justine Wise Polier, who, after retiring in 1973 from the domestic relations court of New York (see chapter 6), ran the CDF program in juvenile justice in 1974, and Marian Wright Edelman, the creator of the Children's Defense Fund. In a 1974 interview Judge Polier said that while "the positive commitment to establish legal rights for children and to secure due process for them in the courts is welcome," she had become involved in the CDF in part because of "the denial of basic and equal services still omnipresent in America's treatment of its children and youth."[64]

Marian Wright Edelman began as an attorney in the civil rights movement and directed the Jackson, Mississippi, office of the NAACP Legal Defense and Education Fund. She was one of the principal architects of the Comprehensive Child Care Act of 1971 and has become one of the leading advocates for all children. According to Edelman, the CDF is "an attempt to create a viable, long-range institution to bring about reforms for children. If they . . . [are] to receive fair treatment and recognition in this country, children require the same kind of planned, systematic, and sustained advocacy, legal and otherwise, that the NAACP Legal Defense and Education Fund, for example, instigated for blacks three decades or more ago."[65]

In 1974 the CDF selected six areas for emphasis: (1) exclusion of children from school (with particular reference to retarded and handicapped children excluded from the public schools before passage of the 1975 Education for All Handicapped Children Act) (PL 94–142); (2) classification and treatment of children with special needs; (3) the use of children in medical research and experimentation; (4) children's right to privacy; (5) reform of the juvenile justice system; and (6) child development and day care.[66]

The CDF was born out of frustration with political interference in the Head Start program in Mississippi in the late 1960s. Working in Jackson, Edelman lamented "the lack of a Washington-based advocate who could anticipate, police, and counter the moves by Senator Stennis and others." Instead, "people who should have been concentrating on children spent inordinate amounts of time trying to survive political attacks."[67]

In 1988 Edelman was still active in the CDF, still working, as she had said in 1974, for "a more responsive and decent country for children to live in." But her 14 years of tireless effort on behalf of the country's children has still left much to do. Indeed, the U.S. infant mortality rate has *increased* during that period. "How can we lead credibly in a world in which the majority of people are nonwhite and poor and looking for moral, social, and economic leadership," she asks, "when we lack the moral and political will to make the American dream real for our own poor children and families." The realities for many American children in 1988 were grim. According to the CDF, only 16 percent of the children needing Head Start actually took part in it. The United States ranked nineteenth in the world with its infant mortality rate of 11 per 1,000 live births. (The rate for African-Americans was 19 per 1,000 in 1988.) And so on.[68]

Conclusion

The children's rights movement is a social movement with no clear beginning and no obvious end in sight. It can be argued that in some respects the movement began in the seventeenth century, or even before, and has continued to the present. The thread holding many disparate social actions together is a concern for and action on behalf of society's children. Sometimes the fix has been worse than the malady, and sometimes the fix itself has had to be fixed many times. Still, the children's rights movement has had some successes. In 1983, for example, M. D. A. Freeman, an attorney, observed that "children today are freer than they were fifty or a hundred years ago; they even have greater autonomy than in previous permissive ages such as the eighteenth century. At no other time in history could a children's liberation movement have flourished."[1]

The ACLU continues to work on cases involving children and their rights. For example, when she was two years old, Sheila A. came under the control of the Kansas Department of Social and Rehabilitation Services (SRS) in March 1988 because of "allegations that her father had severely beaten her half sister." But only nine months later, "SRS returned Sheila to her parents without any assurance that circumstances had changed." Sheila's former foster parents took her to a doctor who "reported that she believed that Sheila had been sexually abused and should be removed from the home and placed in a safe environment." The ACLU is involved in the case because, "although SRS has acknowledged that Sheila's father is dangerous and her home is not safe, it has not removed her or taken steps to protect her."

Another case involves four siblings, Bill, Martin, Laura, and Vincent A. of New York City; they "lived with their mother, who loved them." But she "became involved in a relationship with an abusive man, who beat her." After she was hospitalized, the children were placed separately into foster care. When Ms. A. left the hospital, her children were not returned to her "because she had lost her apartment. The child welfare agency gave her no help in setting up a new household, or in getting counselling about her propensity to become involved with abusive men." After a Children's Rights Project lawsuit was filed, the A. children were reunited four years later.

The ACLU formally withdrew from yet another lawsuit, *In Re: Michele and Michael P.,* because it had finally succeeded in reforming the practices of the Kentucky Department for Social Services regarding adoptions of abused or neglected children. The ACLU had filed the suit with "a novel petition for child neglect against the local department of social services for failing to arrange for adoptions of children in the department's custody for whom adoption had been determined to be appropriate." The Children's Rights Project of the ACLU claimed "that the foster care system itself was harming children in its custody by its failure to carry out placement plans for them, and was therefore a neglectful 'parent.'" The ACLU and the state agency reached agreement, and the court approved a consent decree in September 1981. In spite of this positive result, the agency continued with its old practices. "After the Project obtained two findings of contempt of court, the state began following the requirements of the consent decree, resulting in dramatic improvement." The ACLU concluded that "litigation can be successful in changing the behavior of state foster care agencies."[2]

Thus, lawsuits continue. Cases go on for years, and new issues arise as old ones are settled—or the same old issues arise over and over again. In one sense, the ACLU is simply using the courts to try to force official agencies to live up to the laws that are supposed to govern their behavior. Some agencies that supposedly exist to protect children and act in their best interests turn out to be harmful to those they are chartered to serve. This irony is not new—the history of the juvenile court is a case in point—but it does suggest that the children's rights movement will have a great deal to do for some time to come.

The Children's Defense Fund continues its efforts to make the American system more responsive to the needs of children, and the national and local media continue to note cases of child abuse, neglect, homelessness, and even starvation. Republican efforts for the last 22 years have reduced or reversed the efforts of the children's rights movement to win some basic decency for the nation's youngest and poorest citizens. The child protectionists want to expand the protective agencies, and expand their reach as well. Child liberationists, perhaps frustrated by the long history of ineffectual efforts to protect children, wish to grant full or nearly full autonomy to them. Still others would use the courts to force the child welfare system—always underfunded and understaffed—to live up to its chartered purposes. But all these advocates face a long and difficult struggle in the 1990s, when Americans seem to prefer lower taxes (even in the faces of mounting deficits mainly attributable to unchecked spending on military hardware, largesse, and manpower) over responding to the appeals of abandoned, neglected, abused, mistreated, or exploited children.

Chronology

1641 Massachusetts adopts the *Body of Liberties,* which prescribes capital punishment for rebellious children over 16 but also allows children to defend themselves against abuse.

1646 *Body of Liberties* is modified to provide that rebellious children be brought to court. Virginia passes "binding out" statute allowing local authorities to remove children from their homes without parental consent.

1681 Maryland passes a law requiring special juries to look after the property interests of orphans.

1696 Maryland requires guarantees (bonds) from parents as well as other guardians in orphan's courts; Maryland also extends jurisdiction of orphan's courts to cover all orphans, including those whose father left a will.

1729 Orphan home is established at Ursuline Convent in New Orleans, the first in the United States.

1737 Selectmen of Watertown, Massachusetts, warn some families to place out their children because they are being brought up in "idleness, ignorance, and ereligion [*sic*]."

1739 George Whitefield establishes Bethesda orphanage in Georgia.

1813 Connecticut passes a law requiring some schooling for factory-employed children.

1825 New York House of Refuge is founded, the first U.S. institution for juvenile delinquents.

1831 In *Commonwealth* v. *M'Keagy* the Court of Common Pleas in Philadelphia releases an inmate of a juvenile reformatory because he does not fit statutory requirements, raising the issue of the constitutionality of legislation providing for confinement of youthful offenders.

1839 In *Ex parte Crouse* the Pennsylvania Supreme Court upholds legality of institutions for juvenile delinquents and the right of courts to commit children over parental objections.

1852 Massachusetts passes the first compulsory school attendance law.

1853 Charles Loring Brace founds the New York Children's Aid Society. New York City passes a truancy law; families cannot receive relief unless their children are in school.

1874 New York passes a compulsory school attendance law.

1875 Society for the Prevention of Cruelty to Children is founded.

1882 New York passes Factory Act, which prohibits factory work by children under 13.

1889 American Pediatric Society is founded. Jane Addams founds Hull House.

1892 Kate Douglas Wiggin publishes *Children's Rights*. Zilpha Smith organizes classes for social workers in Boston.

1896 John Dewey founds laboratory school at University of Chicago.

1899 Illinois passes first juvenile court law. John Dewey publishes *School and Society*.

1904 National Child Labor Committee and New York School of Philanthropy are founded. G. Stanley Hall publishes *Adolescence*.

1906 In *Commonwealth* v. *Fisher* the Pennsylvania Supreme Court upholds legality of the juvenile court.

1909 First White House Conference on the Care of Dependent Children recommends the creation of the U.S. Children's

Bureau; also recommends that poverty alone not be used as a reason for removing children from families.

1911 Triangle Shirtwaist Company fire kills 140.

1912 U.S. Children's Bureau is created.

1915 William A. Healy publishes *The Individual Delinquent.*

1916 Congress passes the Keating-Owen Act, the first federal child labor law.

1918 In *Hammer* v. *Dagenhart* the Supreme Court declares Keating-Owen Act unconstitutional. Laura Spelman Rockefeller Memorial, which would be instrumental in supporting child-rearing experts, is founded.

1921 Congress passes Sheppard-Towner Act, a federal-state program to reduce infant mortality.

1922 Congress, with support from the Children's Bureau, and organized labor, recommends a federal anti–child labor amendment, which is strongly opposed by factory owners and many others, including farmers.

1929 Sheppard-Towner Act is ended because of active opposition of the American Medical Association.

1933 Congress passes National Recovery Act codes, which prohibits child labor for children under 16.

1934 Children's Bureau presents a staff study, "Security for Children," that will become the basis for part of the Social Security Act.

1935 Congress passes the Social Security Act, which includes programs for grants to states for Aid to Dependent Children (ADC), maternal and child health programs, crippled children's programs, and child welfare services. National Youth Administration created to employ students and needy youth. In *Shechter Poultry Corporation* v. *United States* the Supreme Court finds National Industrial Recovery Act unconstitutional, thus abolishing codes and the prohibition against child labor.

1938 Congress passes Fair Labor Standards Act, the first permanent federal child labor bill.

1940 White House Conference on Children in a Democracy considers inequalities among children.

1941 In *United States* v. *Darby* the Supreme Court finds Fair Labor Standards Act to be constitutional. Congress passes Community Facilities Act (Lanham Act) to provide federal funds for impact on local communities.

1942 Lanham Act is interpreted to include day care.

1943 "Zoot suit" riots occur in Los Angeles. Congress appropriates funds for Emergency Maternal and Infant Care Program (EMIC) for enlisted men's families.

1946 "Baby boom" begins.

1949 EMIC program is ended.

1951 Congress passes Federal Youth Correction Act, which follows youth authority precepts and prescribes the goal of rehabilitation and the use of parole in federal corrections administration. ADC now assists 1.6 million children.

1953 U.S. Department of Health, Education, and Welfare is created.

1954 In *Brown* v. *Board of Education* the Supreme Court reverses *Plessy* v. *Ferguson* (1896) and rules that the "separate but equal" doctrine under which states maintained segregated schools is unconstitutional. *Seduction of the Innocent* published by Frederick Wertham, who says crime comics cause juvenile delinquency. Comic-book publishers adopt a voluntary code to eliminate obscenity, vulgarity, and horror from comics.

1955 Sen. Estes Kefauver, assumes chair of Senate Subcommittee to Investigate Juvenile Delinquency and begins hearings on the causes of delinquency.

1960 African-American students stage a sit-in to desegregate a lunch counter in Greensboro, North Carolina. Legal Aid Society begins pilot program of having children in New York City juvenile courts represented by lawyers.

1960–1961 Arkansas, Georgia, Michigan, Mississippi, Texas, and Virginia adopt "suitable home" test for ADC recipients.

1961 Congress passes law eliminating suitable home test. C. Henry Kempe, M.D. conducts a symposium in which he proposes the use of the term "battered child syndrome."

1962   Children's Bureau sponsors a conference on child abuse that leads to legislation requiring the reporting of cases of child abuse. New York passes the Family Court Act requiring lawyers for children in formal hearings before the state's family courts.

1963   Betty Friedan publishes *The Feminine Mystique*.

1966   In *Kent* v. *United States* the Supreme Court finds fault with proceedings in juvenile court, anticipating the *Gault* case.

1967   In *In re Gault* the Supreme Court finds that indeterminate sentence for a 15-year-old boy violates due process and requires that juvenile courts provide equal protection of the laws to juveniles.

1968   Congress passes Juvenile Delinquency Prevention and Control Act to assist courts, correctional systems, schools, and community agencies dealing with juvenile delinquency.

1970   Congress passes Education of the Handicapped Act, which combines programs for training teachers and educating handicapped children.

1971   In *McKeiver* v. *Pennsylvania* Supreme Court holds that trial by jury is not a constitutional right in juvenile courts. President Nixon vetoes Comprehensive Child Care Act.

1972   In *Pennsylvania Association for Retarded Children (PARC)* v. *Commonwealth of Pennsylvania,* the Supreme Court agrees that denying schooling to handicapped children is unconstitutional.

1973   Joseph Goldstein, Anna Freud, and Albert Solnit publish *Beyond the Best Interests of the Child.* Children's Defense Fund is established. Congress passes Child Abuse Prevention and Treatment Act, which requires states to meet federal standards on custody provisions, one of which grants state child welfare agencies the power to remove a child from a family for three days if the agency believes the child is in danger; law also creates the National Center on Child Abuse and Neglect, a clearinghouse for reports and information.

1974 Special issue of *Harvard Educational Review* (interviews with Marian Wright Edelman and Justine Wise Polier). Richard Farson publishes *Birthrights*. John Holt publishes *Escape from Childhood*.

1975 Congress passes Education for All Handicapped Children Act (P.L. 94–142), which requires public schools to provide education for handicapped children.

1977 Seattle begins pilot project for use of lay court-appointed special advocates (CASAs).

1979 *Children's Legal Rights Journal* begins publication.

1980 Congress passes Adoption Assistance and Child Welfare Act, which limits the use of foster care.

1981 In *Lassiter* v. *Department of Social Services* the Supreme Court decides that indigent parents facing the loss of their children are not entitled to have a lawyer appointed for them.

1982 In *Santosky* v. *Kramer* the Supreme Court holds that when parental rights are about to be severed, the standard of proof has to be "clear and convincing" rather than "a preponderance of the evidence."

1984 *Doe* v. *Matava* is settled and agreement is reached between the plaintiffs and the state welfare agency that they will work together to improve the Massachusetts system in its work on behalf of neglected and abused children.

1985 *Child Advisory and Protection Newsletter* begins publication.

1988 United States ranks nineteenth among nations of the world in infant mortality rates.

1990 American Civil Liberties Union begins litigation on behalf of victims of child welfare services as a part of its children's rights project.

Notes and References

Preface

1. C. Henry Kempe and others, "The Battered Child Syndrome," *Journal of the American Medical Association* 181 (1962):17–24.

2. N. Ray Hiner, "Children's Rights, Corporal Punishment, and Child Abuse," *Bulletin of the Menninger Clinic* 43 (1979):233–48; Elizabeth Pleck, *Domestic Tyranny: The Making of Social Policy against Family Violence from Colonial Times to the Present* (New York: Oxford University Press, 1987); John R. Sutton, *Stubborn Children: Controlling Delinquency in the United States, 1640–1981* (Berkeley: University of California Press, 1988); and Linda Gordon, *Heroes of Their Own Lives: The Politics and History of Family Violence, Boston, 1880–1960* (New York: Viking, 1988).

3. Michael Grossberg, *Governing the Hearth: Law and the Family in Nineteenth-Century America* (Chapel Hill: University of North Carolina Press, 1985).

Chapter One

1. William Gouge, *Of Domesticall Duties* (London, 1622), quoted in John Demos, *A Little Commonwealth: Family Life in Plymouth Colony* (New York: Oxford University Press, 1970), frontispiece.

2. Chancellor James Kent, *Commentaries on American Law,* 4 vols. (New York: 1826–30), quoted in Grace Abbott, *The Child and the State,* vol. 1, *Legal Status in the Family, Apprenticeship, and Child Labor* (Chicago: University of Chicago Press, 1949), 49–52. Kent is following Sir William Blackstone's *Commentaries,* published in the eighteenth century.

3. Demos, *Little Commonwealth,* 94–95.

4. Ibid., 100, 104–6, 144.

5. James Axtell, *The School upon a Hill: Education and Society in Colonial New England* (New York: W. W. Norton, 1976), 140.

6. Peter Gregg Slater, *Children in the New England Mind in Death and Life* (Hamden, Conn.: Archon Books, 1977), 21–22, 27.

7. John Robinson (*Works of John Robinson*, vol. 1 [Boston, 1851], 250), quoted in Axtell, *School upon a Hill*, 145; Cotton Mather, *Magnalia Christi Americana; or, The Ecclesiastical History of New England* (Hartford, Conn.: Silas Andrews, 1820), 340.

8. Quoted in Robert Bremner, et al. *Children and Youth in America: A Documentary History, 1600–1865*, vol. 1 (Cambridge, Mass.: Harvard University Press, 1970), 38. See also Sutton, *Stubborn Children*, 10.

9. Quoted in Pleck, *Domestic Tyranny*, 21–22.

10. "Records of the Suffolk County Court, 1671–1680," *Colonial Society of Massachusetts Collections* 29 (1933), 478–79.

11. Edmund S. Morgan, *The Puritan Family: Religion and Domestic Relations in Seventeenth-Century New England* (New York: Harper & Row, 1966).

12. Ross Beales, "The Child in Seventeenth Century America," in *American Childhood: A Research Guide and Historical Handbook*, ed. Joseph M. Hawes and N. Ray Hiner (Westport, Conn.: Greenwood Press, 1985), 34–35.

13. William Walter Hening, comp., *The Statutes at Large: Being a Collection of All the Laws of Virginia, from the First Session of the Legislature in the Year 1619*, vol. 1 (New York: R.&W.&G. Bartow, 1823), 157.

14. "Watertown Records Comprising the Third Book of Town Proceedings and the Second Book of Births, Marriages, and Deaths to the End of 1737," quoted in Abbott, *Child and State*, vol. 2, *The Dependent and Delinquent Child*, 212–13.

15. Beales, "Child in Seventeenth Century America," 39–40. According to Beales, "The large numbers of orphans (defined in the Chesapeake as children who had lost their fathers) and the prospect of early death prompted several responses. Acknowledging the odds against a long life and recognizing that stepfathers and guardians might not adequately care for a fatherless child, fathers attempted to ensure their children's well being. They frequently deeded cattle to their sons at birth and appointed trustees to see that the children received the cattle's female increase at marriage or majority; as a result orphans were among the principal owners of cattle in Virginia. . . . The Chesapeake colonies developed mechanisms to guard both orphans and their property" (39–40).

16. Lois Green Carr and Lorena S. Walsh, "The Planter's Wife: The Experience of White Women in Seventeenth-Century Maryland," *William and Mary Quarterly* 34 (October 1977), reprinted in Michael Gordon, ed., *The American Family in Social-Historical Perspective*, 3d ed. (New York: St. Martin's Press, 1983), 331–32.

17. Demos, *Little Commonwealth*, 122–24.

18. "George Whitfield's Journals" (London, 1960), reprinted in Bremner, et al., *Children and Youth in America*, 1:272.

19. Journal of Col. William Stephens, *Georgia Colonial Records*, supple-

ment 4 (1908), reprinted in Bremner, et al., *Children and Youth in America,* vol. 1:273.

Chapter Two

1. Slater, *Children in New England Mind,* 138–48.

2. David Rothman, *The Discovery of the Asylum: Social Order and Disorder in the New Republic* (Boston: Little, Brown, 1971), 213.

3. For a discussion of the relationship between romanticism and children in nineteenth-century America, see Bernard Wishy, *The Child and the Republic: The Dawn of Modern American Child Nurture* (Philadelphia: University of Pennsylvania Press, 1968), Part 2, "The Child Redeemer," as well as Judith Plotz, "The Perpetual Messiah: Romanticism, Childhood, and the Paradoxes of Human Development," and Sterling Fishman, "The Double Vision of Education in the Nineteenth Century: The Romantic and the Grotesque," in Barbara Finkelstein, ed., *Regulated Children/Liberated Children: Education in Psychohistorical Perspective* (New York: Psychohistory Press, 1979), 63–95; 96–113.

4. Bremner, et al., *Children and Youth in America,* 435.

5. Stanley Schultz, *The Culture Factory: Boston Public Schools, 1789–1860* (New York: Oxford University Press, 1973), 69.

6. Ibid., 264–71.

7. Quoted in Joseph M. Hawes, *Children in Urban Society: Juvenile Delinquency in the Nineteenth Century* (New York: Oxford University Press, 1971), 38.

8. Quoted in Bremner, et al., *Children and Youth in America,* 1:681.

9. Quoted in Hawes, *Children in Urban Society,* 58.

10. Quoted in ibid., 59.

11. Quoted in Hawes, *Children in Urban Society,* 91. See also Christine Stansell, *City of Women: Sex and Class in New York, 1789–1860* (Urbana and Chicago: University of Illinois Press, 1987), 198ff.

12. Stansell, *City of Women,* 200.

13. Quoted in Hawes, *Children in Urban Society,* 91.

14. Ibid., 97–98.

15. Stansell, *City of Women,* 207–8.

16. Ibid., 210.

17. Stansell sees this action as essentially class-bound and comments, "The organization considered the separation of parents and children a positive good, the liberation of basically innocent, if somewhat tarnished children from the tyranny of irredeemable adults" (*City of Women,* 210).

18. Ibid., 215.

19. Pleck, *Domestic Tyranny,* 69–75.

20. Quoted in Bremner, et al., *Children and Youth in America,* 196.

21. Quoted in Pleck, *Domestic Tyranny,* 76.

22. Ibid., 79.

23. Quoted in ibid., 83.

24. Ibid., 84–85.

25. Homer Folks, *Care of Destitute, Dependent, and Delinquent Children* (New York: Macmillan, 1902), quoted in Bremner, et al., vol. 2, *1866–1932*, 213–14.

26. Sherri Broder, "Informing 'the Cruelty': The Monitoring of Respectability in Philadelphia's Working Class Neighborhoods in the Late Nineteenth Century," *Radical America* 21 (July–August 1987):36, 41.

27. Gordon, "Family Violence," 26.

28. See Gordon, "Family Violence," 28, but note Pleck's point that most children were *not* removed from their families.

Chapter Three

1. Anthony Platt, *The Child Savers: The Invention of Delinquency* (Chicago: University of Chicago Press, 1969).

2. Viviana A. Zelizer, *Pricing the Priceless Child: The Changing Social Value of Children* (New York: Basic Books, 1985), 28, 211.

3. Wishy, *Child and Republic,* 85.

4. Kate Douglas Wiggin, *Children's Rights* (Boston: Houghton Mifflin, 1892), 11, 19.

5. Burton Bledstein, *The Culture of Professionalism: The Middle Class and the Development of Higher Education in America* (New York: W. W. Norton & Co., 1976), 86.

6. Ibid., 86–87.

7. Edward G. Boring, *A History of Experimental Psychology* (New York: D. Appleton Co., 1935), 324.

8. James Mark Baldwin, *Mental Development in the Child and the Race* (New York: Macmillan, 1894), ix.

9. John Dewey, *School and Society* (Chicago: University of Chicago Press, 1900), 53, 323, 324.

10. John Dewey, "The Psychological Aspect of the School Curriculum," *Educational Review* (April 1897):364–66.

11. Edward L. Thorndike, *Educational Psychology* (New York: Lemche and Beuchner, 1913), 3, 44–45.

12. Ibid., 94, 123, 151.

13. Hawes, *Children in Urban Society,* 202.

14. William T. Stead, *If Christ Came to Chicago* (Chicago: Laird and Lee, 1894), 1, 386.

15. Hawes, *Children in Urban Society,* 158–69.

16. Illinois *Revised Statutes* (1903), 132–37. Conveniently, this act can be found in Abbott, *Child and State,* 2:392.

17. Illinois *Revised Statutes,* 261.

18. Hawes, *Children in Urban Society,* 172, 188.

19. Quoted in Steven Schlossman, *Love and the American Delinquent: The Theory and Practice of "Progressive" Juvenile Justice, 1825–1920* (Chicago: University of Chicago Press, 1977), 160–61.

20. Schlossman, *Love and American Delinquent,* 168–69.

21. Quoted in Merle Curti, *Social Ideas of American Educators* (Totowa, N.J.: Littlefield and Adams, 1968), 496.

22. Dominick Cavallo, "The Politics of Latency: Kindergarten Pedagogy, 1860–1930," in Finkelstein, *Regulated Children/Liberated Children,* 163.

23. Ibid., 170.

24. Wiggin, *Children's Rights,* 228, 235.

Chapter Four

1. Daniel T. Rodgers, "Socializing Middle-Class Children: Institutions, Fables, and Work Values in Nineteenth-Century America," in N. Ray Hiner and Joseph Hawes, eds., *Growing up in America: Children in Historical Perspective* (Urbana and Chicago: University of Illinois Press, 1985). For an account of Brace and the Children's Aid Society, see Hawes, *Children in Urban Society,* 87–111.

2. For a discussion of attitudes about poverty in the United States in the nineteenth century, see Walter I. Trattner, *From Poor Law to Welfare State: A History of Social Welfare in America* (New York: Free Press, 1974).

3. Jane Addams, "The Subtle Problems of Charity," *Atlantic Monthly* 83 (February 1899):170.

4. Walter I. Trattner, *Crusade for the Children: A History of the National Child Labor Committee and Child Labor Reform in America* (Chicago: Quadrangle Books, 1970), 27.

5. Ibid., 29.

6. Ibid., 30.

7. Jeremy Felt, *Hostages of Fortune: Child Labor Reform in New York State* (Syracuse, N.Y.: Syracuse University Press, 1965), 9.

8. Quoted in Dorothy Rose Blumberg, *Florence Kelley: The Making of a Social Pioneer* (New York: Augustus M. Kelley, 1966), 128.

9. Quoted in Allen F. Davis, *American Heroine: The Life and Legend of Jane Addams* (New York: Oxford University Press, 1973), 77.

10. Felt, *Hostages of Fortune,* 38–62; Blumberg, *Florence Kelley,* 161–78.

11. Quoted in Trattner, *Crusade,* 59.

12. Ibid., 60.

13. Ibid., 66.

14. Ibid., 72.

15. Ibid., 74–75.

16. Felt, *Hostages of Fortune,* 72–73.

17. Quoted in Bremner, et al., *Children and Youth in America,* 2:614.

18. Trattner, *Crusade,* 84–87.

19. Ibid., 87–93.

20. Bremner, et al., *Children and Youth in America,* 2:757–74.

21. *U.S. Statutes,* 62 Cong. 2 sess. (1911–12), pt. 1, ch. 73, pp. 79–80.

22. Department of Commerce and Labor, *Report on Condition of Woman and Child Wage-Earners in the United States* (Washington, D.C., 1910), 120–23.

23. Bremner, et al., *Children and Youth in America,* 2:640.

24. Trattner, *Crusade,* 105–6.

25. *New York World,* 26 March 1911, quoted in *America Firsthand,* vol. 2, *From Reconstruction to the Present,* ed. Robert D. Marcus and David Burner (New York: St. Martin's Press, 1989), 182–83.

26. Edward Keating, *The Gentleman from Colorado: A Memoir* (Denver: Sage Books, 1964), 347–53.

27. Trattner, *Crusade,* 133–34.

28. *Hammer* v. *Dagenhart,* 247 *U.S.,* 251–81.

29. Trattner, *Crusade,* 140–42.

30. *Bailey, Collector of Internal Revenue* v. *Drexel Furniture Company,* 259 *U.S. Reports* 20–44.

31. Trattner, *Crusade,* 159; see also Lawrence A. Cremin, *The Transformation of the School* (New York: Alfred A. Knopf, 1961), 127–28.

32. Trattner, *Crusade,* 191–93.

33. Helen Wood, *Young Workers and Their Jobs in 1936,* U.S. Children's Bureau Publication no. 249 (Washington, D.C.: Government Printing Office, 1940), 3–10.

34. Roosevelt to Courtenay Dinwiddie (Secretary, National Child Labor Committee), 8 November 1934, quoted in Bremner, et al., *Children and Youth in America,* vol. 3, *1933–1973,* 325.

35. See Bremner, et al., *Children and Youth in America,* 3:341–47.

Chapter Five

1. Grace Abbott, "Administration of the Sheppard-Towner Act: Plans for Maternal Care," *Transactions of the American Child Hygiene Association* 13 (1922), 194–201.

2. Sheila Rothman, *Woman's Proper Place: A History of Changing Ideals and Practices, 1870 to the Present* (New York: Basic Books, 1978), 137–39. For a discussion of the workings of Sheppard-Towner on the local level, see Elissa Miller, "A History of Nursing Education in Arkansas," Ph.D. dissertation, Memphis State University, 1989.

3. *Congressional Record,* 67 Cong. 1 sess. (1921), 61, pt. 9, 8759–67.

4. David Nasaw, *Children of the City at Work and at Play* (Garden City, N.Y.: Anchor/Doubleday, 1985), 20.

5. Ibid., 27.

6. William A. Healy, *The Individual Delinquent: A Textbook of Diagnosis and Prognosis for All Concerned in Understanding Offenders* (Boston: Little, Brown, 1915). See also Hawes, *Children in Urban Society,* 250–53.

7. Quoted in Hawes, *Children in Urban Society,* 253 (emphasis in original).

8. William A. Healy, *Mental Conflicts and Misconduct* (Boston: Little, Brown, 1917), 2–3, 6, 7–8, 17, 19–20, 22–24, 30–31, 54, 71–72, 75–76, 316–17, 321, 325.

9. Hamilton Cravens, "Child Saving in the Age of Professionalism, 1915–1930," in Hawes and Hiner, *American Childhood,* 417.

10. Geraldine Joncich, ed., *Psychology and the Science of Education: Selected Writings of Edward L. Thorndike* (New York: Bureau of Publications, Teachers College, Columbia University, 1962), 148. The Binet Intelligence Test is named for Alfred Binet, French psychologist. It was first published in the United States by Henry H. Goddard in 1910. Cravens, "Child Saving," 427.

11. Cravens, "Child Saving," 427.

12. Ibid., 436.

13. See the excellent discussion of Gesell in Hawes and Hiner, *American Childhood,* 428–29.

14. Lawrence A. Cremin, *American Education: The Metropolitan Experience, 1876–1980* (New York: Harper and Row, 1988), 289.

15. Quoted in Rothman, *Woman's Proper Place,* 106 (emphasis in original).

16. Cravens, "Child Saving," 449.

17. Christopher Lasch, *Haven in a Heartless World: The Family Besieged* (New York: Basic Books, 1977), xxi.

18. Douglas A. Thom, "Habit Clinics for Children of the Pre-School Age," *American Journal of Psychiatry* 79 (1922–23), reprinted in Bremner, et al., *Children and Youth in America,* 2:1052.

19. Christopher Lasch, *The Culture of Narcissism: American Life in an Age of Diminishing Expectations* (New York: Warner Books, 1979), 279n.

20. Paula Fass, *The Damned and the Beautiful: American Youth in the 1920s* (New York: Oxford University Press, 1979), 6.

21. Beth L. Bailey, *From Front Porch to Back Seat: Courtship in Twentieth-Century America* (Baltimore: Johns Hopkins University Press, 1988), 17.

22. John Modell, *Into One's Own: From Youth to Adulthood in the United States, 1920–1975* (Berkeley: University of California Press, 1989), 95.

23. See Lasch, *Haven in a Heartless World,* 56–58.

24. Modell, *Into One's Own,* 119.

Chapter Six

1. William E. Leuchtenburg, *Franklin D. Roosevelt and the New Deal, 1932–1940* (New York: Harper and Row, 1963), 1.

2. Studs Terkel, *Hard Times: An Oral History of the Great Depression* (New York: Avon Books, 1970), 62.

3. Ibid., 111, 117. See also Glen Elder, *Children of the Great Depression* (Chicago: University of Chicago Press, 1974), 64.

4. Elder, *Children of Great Depression,* 80.

5. Leuchtenburg, *Roosevelt and New Deal,* 26–29.

6. Ibid., 46–54, 120–24.

7. Maren Strange, "Publicity, Husbandry, and Technology: Fact and Symbol in Civilian Conservation Corps Photography," in Pete Daniel, et al., eds., *Official Images: New Deal Photography* (Washington, D.C.: Smithsonian Institution Press, 1987), 66–70.

8. Sally Stein, "Figures of the Future: Photography of the National Youth Administration," in ibid., 96.

9. Ibid., 97–98.

10. Mary McLeod Bethune to Aubrey Williams, 10 June 1938, NYA records, quoted in Bremner, et al., *Children and Youth in America,* 3:87.

11. Stein, "Figures of the Future," 100–16.

12. Paul B. Jacobson, "End of N.Y.A.," *School Review* 51 (1943):454–56.

13. *Who's Who among American Women,* 3d ed. (Chicago: Marquis, 1964–65).

14. U.S. Children's Bureau, "Security for Children," staff study included in U.S. Committee on Economic Security, *Social Security in America: The Factual Background of the Social Security Act as Summarized from the Staff Reports to the Committee on Economic Security,* Social Security Board publication no. 20 (Washington, D.C., 1937), 229–31.

15. Leroy Ashby, "The Depression and World War II," in Hawes and Hiner, *American Childhood,* 506–7; Robert S. Lynd and Helen Merrell Lynd, *Middletown in Transition: A Study in Cultural Conflicts* (New York: Harcourt Brace, 1937).

16. F. Jack Hurley, *Portrait of a Decade: Roy Stryker and the Development of Documentary Photography in the Thirties* (Baton Rouge: Louisiana State University Press, 1972), 96–98.

17. All the photographs discussed in this paragraph can be found in Hurley, *Portrait of a Decade.* For a sample of Hine's work, see John R. Kemp, ed., *Lewis Hine: Photographs of Child Labor in the New South* (Jackson: University Press of Mississippi, 1986).

18. Hurley, *Portrait of a Decade,* 122–46.

19. Leuchtenburg, *Roosevelt and New Deal,* 132–33. See also Trattner, *From Poor Law to Welfare State,* 242.

20. Ashby, "Depression and World War II," 496. For an extended discussion of this problem, see "Rights of Children under AFDC," in Bremner, et al., *Children and Youth in America,* 3:576–619.

21. Ashby, "Depression and World War II," 499–500.

22. Bremner, et al., *Children and Youth in America,* 3:722–27.

23. Edna Ewing Kelley, "Uncle Sam's Nursery Schools," *Parents' Magazine* (March 1936):24–25, 48–49.

24. U.S. Federal Works Agency, *Final Report on the WPA Program, 1935–1943* (Washington, D.C., 1947), 61–62.

25. Justine Wise Polier, *Everyone's Children, Nobody's Child* (New York: Charles Scribner's Sons, 1941), 246–50; American Humane Association, *Standards for Child Protection Societies* (Albany, N.Y.: American Humane Association, 1939), 7–9.

26. See, for example, Bremner, et al., *Children and Youth in America,* 3:1008–11.

27. John Forbes Perkins, "Indeterminate Control of Offenders: Arbitrary and Discriminatory," *Law and Contemporary Problems* 9 (Autumn 1942):624–25, 628–31, 634.

28. John Barker White, "Indeterminate Control: Realistic and Protective," *Law and Contemporary Problems* 9 (Autumn 1942):619–23.

29. White House Conference on Children in a Democracy, *Final Report* (Washington, D.C.: Government Printing Office, 1940), 269–71. In 1951 Congress passed the Federal Youth Correction Act, which established the youth authority approach in the federal juvenile justice system (Bremner, et al., *Children and Youth in America,* 3:1991).

Chapter Seven

1. Quoted in Ashby, "Depression and World War II," 511.

2. White House Conference on Children in a Democracy, *Final Report* (Washington, D.C.: 1940), 269–71.

3. James Gilbert, *A Cycle of Outrage: America's Reaction to the Juvenile Delinquent in the 1950s* (New York: Oxford University Press, 1986), 25–26.

4. Gilbert, *Cycle of Outrage,* 36.

5. Ibid., 30–33; for a vivid example of this sort of propaganda, see the film "Rosie the Riveter."

6. Bremner, et al., *Children and Youth in America,* 3:681.

7. Kathryn Close, "Day Care up to Now," *Survey Midmonthly* 79 (July 1943):194–97.

8. Ibid.

9. "Care of Infants Whose Mothers Are Employed: Policies Recommended by the Children's Bureau," *The Child* 9 (1945):131–32.

10. Ashby, "Depression and World War II," 501–3.

11. "Report of Meeting of Maternal and Child Health Advisory Committee of the Children's Bureau," *Journal of the American Medical Association* 122 (1943):845.

12. "The EMIC Program," *Journal of Pediatrics* 25 (1944):88–91.

13. Grover F. Powers, "A Letter to the Editors," *Journal of Pediatrics* 25 (August 1944).

14. Bremner, et al., *Children and Youth in America,* 3:1263–69. See also Dorothy E. Bradbury, *Five Decades of Action for Children: A History of the Children's Bureau* (Washington, D.C.: Government Printing Office, 1962).

15. For a definition of the family ideal, see Pleck, *Domestic Tyranny,* 7–11. For a discussion of family life in the postwar years, see Elaine Tyler May, *Homeward Bound: American Families in the Cold War Era* (New York: Basic Books, 1988).

16. Landon Jones, *Great Expectations: America and the Baby Boom Generation* (New York: Ballantine Books, 1986), 23–24.

17. Margaret O'Brien Steinfels, *Who's Minding the Children: The History and Politics of Day Care in America* (New York: Simon and Schuster, 1973), 70.

18. Quoted in Steinfels, *Who's Minding the Children,* 72.

19. Betty Friedan, *The Feminine Mystique* (New York: W. W. Norton, 1963).

20. Steinfels, *Who's Minding the Children,* 74–76.

21. Winifred Bell, *Aid to Dependent Children* (New York: Columbia University Press, 1965), 57–151.

22. Chap. 9, "Mass Media and Delinquency: A National Forum," in Gilbert, *Cycle of Outrage,* is a thorough account of the hearings.

23. Ibid. For a discussion of Comstock, see Hawes, *Children in Urban Society,* 124–25.

24. Gilbert, *Cycle of Outrage,* 149; Bradbury, *Five Decades of Action,* 89.

25. Gilbert, *Cycle of Outrage,* 151–52.

26. Ibid., 159.

27. For a discussion of the rise of policy-oriented social science in the middle of the twentieth century in the United States, see Lasch, *Haven in a Heartless World,* 97ff.

28. Ellen Ryerson, *The Best-Laid Plans: America's Juvenile Court Experiment* (New York: Hill and Wang, 1978), 142–44. See also Sutton, *Stubborn Children,* ch. 6, "In Need of Supervision."

29. Gilbert, *Cycle of Outrage,* 195.

Chapter Eight

1. Rothman, *Woman's Proper Place,* 232.

2. Jane E. Knitzer, "Child Advocacy: A Perspective," *American Journal of Orthopsychiatry* 46 (April 1976):201.

3. For an overview of the entire issue of children's rights, see Thomas A. Nazario, *In Defense of Children: Understanding the Rights, Needs, and Interests of the Child* (New York: Charles Scribner's Sons, 1988); see also Jane Knitzer, "Children's Rights in the Family and Society: Dilemmas and Realities," *American Journal of Orthopsychiatry* 52 (July 1982):481–95.

4. Friedan, *Feminine Mystique,* 226–28. Even as Friedan wrote, women were increasing their participation in the work force and undermining the very

basis for the "feminine mystique." For a more recent study of the same problem, see May, *Homeward Bound.*

5. Rothman, *Woman's Proper Place,* 235, 243.

6. Ibid., 246–47.

7. Joseph Goldstein, Anna Freud, and Albert Solnit, *Beyond the Best Interests of the Child* (New York: Free Press, 1973), 17, 19; Selma Fraiberg, *Every Child's Birthright: In Defense of Mothering* (New York: Basic Books, 1977). See also Rothman, *Woman's Proper Place,* ch. 6.

8. Bradbury, *Five Decades of Action,* 119. See also Department of Health, Education, and Welfare, Social Security Administration, Children's Bureau, *It's Your Children's Bureau* (Washington, D.C.: Government Printing Office, 1963).

9. Samuel X. Radbill, "A History of Child Abuse and Infanticide," in *The Battered Child,* ed. Ray E. Helfer and C. Henry Kempe (Chicago: University of Chicago Press, 1968), 15–17; Kempe, et al., "Battered Child Syndrome," 17–19, 20–21, 23–24.

10. Pleck, *Domestic Tyranny,* 169–73. See also Richard J. Light, "Abused and Neglected Children in America: A Study of Alternative Policies," *Harvard Educational Review* 43 (November 1973):556–98.

11. Light, "Abused and Neglected Children," 587–88.

12. David C. Gil, *Violence against Children: Physical Child Abuse in the United States* (Cambridge, Mass.: Harvard University Press, 1970), 133–48.

13. Pleck, *Domestic Tyranny,* 175–77.

14. Douglas J. Basharov, "Unfounded Allegations—A New Child Abuse Problem," *Public Interest* 83 (Spring 1986):19.

15. Robert Mnookin, "Foster Care—in Whose Best Interest?" *Harvard Educational Review* 43 (November 1973):604.

16. Ibid., 606, 609.

17. Ibid., 615.

18. Ibid., 617–19.

19. Goldstein, Freud, and Solnit, *Beyond Best Interests,* 19.

20. Ibid., 25.

21. Ibid., pt. 2, 31–67.

22. A second edition of *Beyond the Best Interests of the Child* was published in 1979. See the discussion of their recommendations in Pleck, *Domestic Tyranny,* 179–80.

23. Alene Byer Russell and Cynthia Trainor, *Trends in Child Abuse and Neglect: A National Perspective* (Denver: American Humane Association, 1984), 7–23.

24. Ibid., 40–42.

25. *Kent* v. *United States,* 383 U.S. 541 (1966); Ryerson, *Best-Laid Plans,* 148–50.

26. Peter S. Prescott, *The Child Savers: Juvenile Justice Observed* (New York: Alfred A. Knopf, 1981), 59–60, 65.

27. Sutton, *Stubborn Children,* 201.

28. *In re Gault,* 387 U.S. 1 (1967).

29. Ibid.

30. Ryerson, *Best-Laid Plans,* 151. In 1968 Congress passed the Juvenile Delinquency Prevention and Control Act to provide federal assistance to state juvenile justice systems (Bremner, et al., *Children and Youth in America,* 3:1997). In 1971 the Supreme Court found that there was no constitutional right to a trial by jury in a juvenile court (ibid., 1999).

31. Sutton, *Stubborn Children,* 204–18.

32. Ibid., 251.

33. Prescott, *Child Savers,* 244.

34. Ibid.

35. Sutton, *Stubborn Children,* 249–50.

36. Donald N. Bersoff, "From Courthouse to Schoolhouse: Using the Legal System to Secure the Right to an Appropriate Education," *American Journal of Orthopsychiatry* 52 (July 1982): 506–9. For a discussion of similar activity in Massachusetts, see Peter B. Edelman, "The Massachusetts Task Force Reports: Advocacy for Children," *Harvard Educational Review* 43 (November 1973):639–52. For a conservative critique of the process, see John C. Pittenger and Peter Kuriloff, "Educating the Handicapped in Reforming a Radical Law," *Public Interest* 66 (Winter 1982):72–96. Earlier in 1970 Congress had passed the Education of the Handicapped Act that combined teacher training and education in selected school programs for the handicapped (Bremner, et al., *Children and Youth in America,* 3:1998).

37. Quoted in Bersoff, "Courthouse to Schoolhouse," 510.

38. Robert H. Mnookin, *In the Interest of Children: Advocacy Law Reform and Public Policy* (San Francisco: W. H. Freeman and Co., 1985), 10.

39. Gary B. Melton, "Litigation *In the Interest of Children,*" *Law and Human Behavior* 10 (December 1986):342.

40. American Civil Liberties Union, case summaries (May 1990); see also ACLU, "Victims of Child Welfare: A Proposal for Funding"; both available from the ACLU, 132 W. 43d St., New York, NY 10036.

41. Marcia Lowry, "Derring-do in the 1980s: Child Welfare Impact Litigation after the Warren Years," *Family Law Quarterly* 20 (Summer 1986):261.

42. Ibid., 262. For an assessment of the difficulties of litigation during the years of the Burger Court, see Nat Stern, "The Burger Court and the Diminishing Constitutional Rights of Minors: A Brief Overview," *Arizona State Law Review* 50 (November 1985):865–904.

43. Lowry, "Derring-do," 264.

44. Ibid., 265.

45. Ibid., 269–70.

46. Quoted in ibid., 271.

47. Ibid., 273.

48. Ibid., 277–78.

49. Donald N. Duquette and Sarah H. Ramsey, "Representation of Children in Child Abuse and Neglect Cases: An Empirical Look at What Constitutes Effective Representation," *University of Michigan Journal of Law Reform* 20 (Winter 1987):341–408. On the impact of *Gault,* see Henry H. Foster, Jr. and Doris Jonas Freed, "A Bill of Rights for Children," *Family Law Quarterly* 6 (Winter 1972):343–75; Andrew Jay Kleinfeld, "The Balance of Power among Infants, Parents, and the State," *Family Law Quarterly* 2 (September 1970):320–50; and Gail Marker and Paul R. Friedman, "Re-Thinking Children's Rights," *Children Today* 2 (November–December 1973):8–11.

50. "Massachusetts Bar Association Study," *Child Advocacy and Protection Newsletter* 2 (January 1989):n.p.

51. The literature on the emergence of active advocacy on behalf of children in the 1970s is immense. See, for example, Foster and Freed, "A Bill of Rights for Children"; David Gottlieb, ed., *Children's Liberation* (Englewood Cliffs, N.J.: Prentice-Hall, 1973); Beatrice and Ronald Gross, eds., *The Children's Rights Movement: Overcoming the Oppression of Young People* (Garden City, N.Y.: Anchor Books, 1977); Advisory Committee on Child Development, Assembly of Behavioral and Social Sciences, National Research Council, *Toward a National Policy for Children and Families* (Washington, D.C.: National Academy of Sciences, 1977); Kenneth Keniston and the Carnegie Council on Children, *All Our Children: The American Family under Pressure* (New York: Harcourt Brace Jovanovich, 1977); and Kenneth Wooden, *Weeping in the Playtime of Others: America's Incarcerated Children* (New York: McGraw-Hill, 1976).

52. Richard Farson, *Birthrights* (New York: Macmillan, 1974), 1–2, 5.

53. John Holt, *Escape from Childhood* (New York: Ballantine Books, 1974), 1–2.

54. Ibid., 1–2.

55. Howard Cohen, *Equal Rights for Children* (Totowa, N.J.: Littlefield, Adams & Co., 1980), 9–10.

56. Farson, *Birthrights,* 10; Cohen, *Equal Rights,* 11–12.

57. Neal Postman, *The Disappearance of Childhood* (New York: Delacorte Press, 1982), 120–34, 141.

58. Ibid., 141.

59. Farson, *Birthrights,* 8. The literature in support of the protectionist viewpoint is voluminous and expanding. For example, see Children's Defense Fund, *A Call for Action to Make Our Nation Safe for Children: A Briefing Book on the State of American Children in 1988* (Washington, D.C.: Children's Defense Fund, 1988).

60. Lois G. Forer, *No One Will Lissen: How Our Legal System Brutalizes the Youthful Poor* (New York: John Day Co., 1970), 11–12.

61. Stacie G. Goffin and Joan Lombardi, *Speaking out: Early Childhood Advocacy* (Washington, D.C.: National Association for the Education of Young Children, 1988).

62. Edward Zigler and Susan Muenchow, "How to Influence Social Policy Affecting Children and Families," *American Psychologist* 39 (April 1984):415–20. For a discussion of the history of the White House Conferences on Children and Youth, see Rochelle Beck, "The White House Conferences on Children: An Historical Perspective," *Harvard Educational Review* 43 (November 1973):653–68. Beck concludes: "The proceedings of the Conferences read like a history of ideas and programs, with problems seen through the eyes of adults, rather than reports dealing with flesh and blood children. . . . In the sweep of seven decades, the image conveyed is one of children, smaller than anyone else, lighter in physical weight and political clout, easily picked up and blown wherever the winds of economic, political and social movements were heading" (668). As of this writing, no further conference has been held.

63. Judith S. Mearig, "Ethical Implications of the Children's Rights Movement for Professionals," *American Journal of Orthopsychiatry* 52 (July 1982):518–29.

64. "Myths and Realities in the Search for Juvenile Justice: A Statement by the Honorable Justine Wise Polier," *Harvard Educational Review* 44 (February 1974):113.

65. "An Interview with Marian Wright Edelman," *Harvard Educational Review* 44 (February 1974):53–54.

66. Ibid., 54–55.

67. Ibid., 67.

68. Ibid., 73; CDE, "A Call for Action" (1988), vii, 7, 27, 37.

Conclusion

1. M. D. A. Freeman, *The Rights and Wrongs of Children* (London: Frances Pinter, 1983), 16.

2. American Civil Liberties Union, "Victims of Child Welfare: A Proposal for Funding" (1990), and case summaries (May 1990), both available from the American Civil Liberties Union, 132 W. 43d St., New York, NY 10036.

Bibliographic Essay

General

There is as yet no comprehensive history of American children or of American childhood. The best overviews are to be found in Robert Bremner, et al., *Children and Youth in America: A Documentary History*, 3 vols. (Cambridge, Mass.: Harvard University Press, 1970–74); Joseph Hawes and N. Ray Hiner, *American Childhood: A Research Guide and Historical Handbook* (Westport, Conn.: Greenwood Press, 1985); and N. Ray Hiner and Joseph Hawes, *Growing up in America* (Urbana: University of Illinois Press, 1985). An older documentary collection, Grace Abbott's *The Child and the State*, 2 vols. (Chicago: University of Chicago Press, 1938), is still useful. There is no history of children's rights nor of the children's rights movement. Hawes and Hiner's *American Childhood* is primarily a guide to the literature on the history of American childhood and remains the principal reference work in the field.

Chapter One

The best guide to studies on colonial children is the chapter by Ross Beales, "The Child in Seventeenth Century America," in Hawes and Hiner, *American Childhood.* The best recent treatment of children in colonial America is John Demos, *A Little Commonwealth: Family Life in Plymouth Colony* (New York: Oxford University Press, 1970). Also dealing with colonial families, but in a different region, is J. William Frost, *The Quaker Family in Colonial America* (New York: St. Martin's Press, 1973). Particularly useful because of the discussion of the Massachusetts stubborn child law is John R. Sutton, *Stubborn Children: Controlling De-*

linquency in the United States, 1640–1981 (Berkeley: University of California Press, 1988). Other important works dealing with children in colonial America include James Axtell's *The School upon a Hill: Education and Society in Colonial New England* (New York: W. W. Norton, 1976) and the relevant sections of Bremner, et al., *Children and Youth in America* and Abbott, *The Child and the State.* An important and useful article is Lois Green Carr and Lorena S. Walsh, "The Planter's Wife: The Experience of White Women in Seventeenth-Century Maryland," *William and Mary Quarterly* 34 (1977). Other useful discussions include Ross Beales, "Anne Bradstreet and Her Children," in Barbara Finkelstein, ed., *Regulated Children/Liberated Children: Education in Psychohistorical Perspective* (New York: Psychohistory Press, 1979); N. Ray Hiner, "Cotton Mather and His Children," in Finkelstein, *Regulated Children/Liberated Children;* and Ross Beales, "In Search of the Historical Child: Youth and Miniature Adulthood in Colonial New England," *American Quarterly* 27 (October 1975).

Chapter Two

Peter Slater, *Children in the New England Mind in Death and Life* (Hamden, Conn.: Archon Books, 1977), which covers both the colonial and early national periods, traces the evolution of moral and philosophical attitudes toward children from the doctrine of original sin through the Enlightenment view of children as blank slates, to the rise of romanticism. The best treatment of the creation of the urban public school system is Stanley Schultz's *The Culture Factory: Boston Public Schools, 1789–1860* (New York: Oxford University Press, 1973); Michael Katz's *The Irony of Early American School Reform* (Cambridge, Mass.: Harvard University Press, 1968) discusses the relationship between early public schools and the rise of houses of refuge. On juvenile institutions, see Joseph Hawes, *Children in Urban Society: Juvenile Delinquency in the Nineteenth Century* (New York: Oxford University Press, 1971), and Robert Mennel, *Thorns and Thistles: Juvenile Delinquents in the United States, 1825–1940* (Hanover, N.H.: University Press of New England, 1973). Other eleemosynary institutions are treated adequately in David Rothman, *The Discovery of the Asylum: Social Order and Disorder in the New Republic* (Boston: Little, Brown, 1971). The rise of the philanthropic practice of "placing out" children in farm families is described in Hawes, *Children in Urban Society,* but for a more recent and critical view, see Christine Stansell, *City of Women: Sex and Class in New York,*

1789–1860 (Urbana and Chicago: University of Illinois Press, 1987). The urban response to child abuse, including the creation of the Society for the Prevention of Cruelty to Children, is described in Elizabeth Pleck, *Domestic Tyranny: The Making of Social Policy against Family Violence from Colonial Times to the Present* (New York: Oxford University Press, 1987); Linda Gordon, *Heroes of Their Own Lives: The Politics and History of Family Violence in Boston, 1880–1960* (New York: Viking, 1988) is similar in scope. For studies of how working-class families dealt with child abuse and the SPCC, see Sherri Broder, "Informing 'the Cruelty': The Monitoring of Respectability in Philadelphia's Working Class Neighborhoods in the Late Nineteenth Century," *Radical America* 5 (July–August 1987), and Linda Gordon, "Family Violence in History and Politics," in the same issue of *Radical America.*

Chapter Three

For a comprehensive overview of child rescue efforts during the Progressive Era, see Anthony Platt, *The Child Savers: The Invention of Delinquency* (Chicago: University of Chicago Press, 1969). Similar in scope but focusing on dependent children alone is Leroy Ashby, *Saving the Waifs: Reformers and Dependent Children, 1890–1917* (Philadelphia: Temple University Press, 1984). For a discussion of the romantic image of children and the idea that children would save society because of their innocence, see Bernard Wishy, *The Child and the Republic: The Dawn of Modern American Child Nurture* (Philadelphia: University of Pennsylvania Press, 1968). To understand how the sentimental value of children increased even as their economic worth declined, see Viviana A. Zelizer, *Pricing the Priceless Child: The Changing Social Value of Children* (New York: Basic Books, 1985). For the romantic view of children's rights, the best source is Kate Douglas Wiggin, *Children's Rights* (Boston: Houghton Mifflin, 1892). The best guide to the process of professionalization is Burton Bledstein, *The Culture of Professionalism: The Middle Class and the Development of Higher Education in America* (New York: W. W. Norton & Co., 1976). For an understanding of G. Stanley Hall and the child study movement, see Dorothy G. Ross, *G. Stanley Hall: The Psychologist as Prophet* (Chicago: University of Chicago Press, 1972). On the early history of psychology, see Edwin G. Boring, *A History of Experimental Psychology* (New York: D. Appleton Co., 1935). John Dewey, *School and Society* (Chicago: University of Chicago Press, 1900) is his primary work explaining his project of psychologizing the schools. Thorndike's views are articulated in Edward L. Thorndike, *Educational Psychology* (New York: Lemche and Beuchner, 1913). Jane Addams's views of the nature of social work are found in Jane Addams, *Spirit of Youth and City Streets* (New York: Macmillan, 1930); an outline of the professionalization of social work can be found in Hawes, *Children in Urban Society*.

The outstanding example of sensational journalism about children is William T. Stead, *If Christ Came to Chicago* (Chicago: Laird and Lee, 1894). The creation of the juvenile court is traced in both Hawes, *Children in Urban Society* and Platt, *The Child Savers*. For a study of actual juvenile court records and the day-to-day workings of the court in the Progressive Era, Steven Schlossman, *Love and the American Delinquent: The Theory and Practice of "Progressive" Juvenile Justice, 1825–1920* (Chicago: University of Chicago Press, 1977) is unexcelled. The clearest account of the early history of the kindergarten and the controversy between the scientific and romantic kindergartners is Dominick Cavallo, "The Politics of Latency: Kindergarten Pedagogy, 1860–1930," in Finkelstein, *Regulated Children/Liberated Children*.

Chapter Four

The standard history of the child labor movement in the United States is Walter I. Trattner's *Crusade for the Children: A History of the National Child Labor Committee and Child Labor Reform in America* (Chicago: Quadrangle Books, 1970), but see also Jeremy Felt, *Hostages of Fortune: Child Labor Reform in New York State* (Syracuse, N.Y.: Syracuse University Press, 1965). On the matter of socializing middle-class children, see Daniel T. Rodgers, "Socializing Middle-Class Children: Institutions, Fables, and Work Values in Nineteenth-Century America," in Hiner and Hawes, *Growing up in America*. For an account of Charles Loring Brace and the Children's Aid Society, see Hawes, *Children in Urban Society*. Two important biographies are Dorothy Rose Blumberg, *Florence Kelley: The Making of a Social Pioneer* (New York: Augustus M. Kelley, 1966), and Allen F. Davis, *American Heroine: The Life and Legend of Jane Addams* (New York: Oxford University Press, 1973). An important general work is Lawrence A. Cremin, *The Transformation of the School* (New York: Alfred A. Knopf, 1961), and also his *American Education: The Metropolitan Experience, 1876–1980* (New York: Harper and Row, 1988). The important cases and legislation can be found in Bremner, et al., *Children and Youth in America*, but both volume 2 (1971) and volume 3

(1974) must be consulted. A very significant Children's Bureau publication is Helen Wood, *Young Workers and Their Jobs in 1936,* U.S. Children's Bureau publication no. 249 (Washington, D.C.: Government Printing Office, 1940).

Chapter Five

An extremely important work on the early twentieth century, including the 1920s, is David Nasaw, *Children of the City at Work and at Play* (Garden City, N.Y.: Anchor/Doubleday, 1985). William A. Healy's primary work is *The Individual Delinquent: A Textbook of Diagnosis and Prognosis for All Concerned in Understanding Offenders* (Boston: Little, Brown, 1915). An account of Healy's early work can be found in Hawes, *Children in Urban Society.* See also Healy's *Mental Conflicts and Misconduct* (Boston: Little, Brown, 1917). Hamilton Cravens, "Child Saving in the Age of Professionalism, 1915–1930," in Hawes and Hiner, *American Childhood,* is more than a guide to the literature; it provides some fresh scholarship on the rise of child science in the period and is particularly important on the role of the Rockefeller Foundation. Very useful for an understanding of the period is Sheila Rothman, *Woman's Proper Place: A History of Changing Ideals and Practices, 1870 to the Present* (New York: Basic Books, 1978). Of major importance for an understanding of the rise of peer groups is Paula Fass, *The Damned and the Beautiful: American Youth in the 1920s* (New York: Oxford University Press, 1979). Other recent works that touch on the period include Beth L. Bailey, *From Front Porch to Back Seat: Courtship in Twentieth-Century America* (Baltimore: Johns Hopkins University Press, 1988), and John Modell, *Into One's Own: From Youth to Adulthood in the United States, 1920–1975* (Berkeley: University of California Press, 1989). Christopher Lasch also explores the rise of the youth culture and discusses the significance of dating in *Haven in a Heartless World: The Family Besieged* (New York: Basic Books, 1977), and *The Culture of Narcissism* (New York: Warner Books, 1979).

Chapter Six

The literature on the Great Depression and the New Deal is voluminous. Handy and quite lucid is William E. Leuchtenberg, *Franklin D. Roosevelt and the New Deal 1932–1940* (New York: Harper and Row, 1963). More recent and very readable is Studs Terkel, *Hard Times: An*

Oral History of the Great Depression (New York: Avon Books, 1970). The most important work on the impact of the Great Depression on the lives of children born during the period is Glen Elder, *Children of the Great Depression* (Chicago: University of Chicago Press, 1974). An important guide to the photography of the New Deal is Pete Daniel, et al., eds., *Official Images: New Deal Photography* (Washington, D.C.: Smithsonian Institution Press, 1987). In that collection, Sally Stein's "Figures of the Future: Photography of the National Youth Administration" is especially useful. On photography of the period, see also F. Jack Hurley, *Portrait of a Decade: Roy Stryker and the Development of Documentary Photography in the Thirties* (Baton Rouge: Louisiana State University Press, 1972). A recent discussion of the work of Lewis Hine is John R. Kemp, ed., *Lewis Hine: Photographs of Child Labor in the New South* (Jackson: University Press of Mississippi, 1986). Leroy Ashby's "The Depression and World War II," in Hawes and Hiner, *American Childhood* is a concise and clear guide to the major literature about children during the period. The classic work on an American community during the depression is Robert S. Lynd and Helen Merrell Lynd, *Middletown in Transition: A Study in Cultural Conflicts* (New York: Harcourt Brace, 1937). A general history that details the development of social welfare legislation in the New Deal is Walter Trattner, *From Poor Law to Welfare State: A History of Social Welfare in America* (New York: Free Press, 1974). The growth of federal day-care centers during the New Deal is treated in Edna Ewing Kelley, "Uncle Sam's Nursery Schools," *Parents' Magazine* (March 1936). The findings of the 1940 conference are in U.S. White House Conference on Children in a Democracy, *Final Report* (Washington, D.C.: Government Printing Office, 1940).

Chapter Seven

Bremner, et al., *Children and Youth in America* is vital for an understanding of developments during World War II. The question of wartime juvenile delinquency and the fears of delinquency after the war are treated very effectively in James Gilbert, *A Cycle of Outrage: America's Reaction to the Juvenile Delinquent in the 1950s* (New York: Oxford University Press, 1986). The role of the Children's Bureau during the war is traced by Dorothy E. Bradbury, *Five Decades of Action for Children: A History of the Children's Bureau* (Washington, D.C.: Government Printing Office, 1962). The plan for prenatal care for the families of enlisted men during the war can be followed in Bremner, et al., *Children and Youth in America*. The best treatment of day care is Margaret O'Brien Steinfels, *Who's Minding the Children: The History and Politics of Day Care in America* (New York: Simon and Schuster, 1973). A clear and concise history of early federal aid programs for children can be found in Winifred Bell, *Aid to Dependent Children* (New York: Columbia University Press, 1965). The baby boom is most easily understood through Landon Jones, *Great Expectations: America and the Baby Boom Generation* (New York: Ballantine Books, 1986). The rise of policy-oriented social science is treated by Christopher Lasch in *Haven in a Heartless World*. On the juvenile court at midcentury, see Ellen Ryerson, *The Best-Laid Plans: America's Juvenile Court Experiment* (New York: Hill and Wang, 1978). Also important on the workings of the juvenile justice system is Sutton, *Stubborn Children*. On families in the period, see Elaine Tyler May, *Homeward Bound: American Families in the Cold War Era* (New York: Basic Books, 1988), and also Pleck, *Domestic Tyranny*.

Chapter Eight

The changing relationship between children's rights advocates and feminists can be traced in Rothman, *Woman's Proper Place*. For an overview of issues in children's rights, see Thomas A. Nazario, *In Defense of Children: Understanding the Rights, Needs, and Interests of the Child* (New York: Charles Scribner's Sons, 1988). A succinct overview is provided by Jane Knitzer, "Children's Rights in the Family and Society: Dilemmas and Realities," *American Journal of Orthopsychiatry* 52 (July 1982). The critique of child placement practices based on the concept of "psychological parenting" is in Joseph Goldstein, Anna Freud, and Albert Solnit, *Beyond the Best Interests of the Child* (New York: Free Press, 1973). For a vigorous defense of an infant's need for mothering, see Selma Fraiberg, *Every Child's Birthright: In Defense of Mothering* (New York: Basic Books, 1977).

The discussion of the medical implications of child abuse can be found in *The Battered Child,* ed. Ray E. Helfer and C. Henry Kempe (Chicago: University of Chicago Press, 1968). See especially Samuel X. Radbill, "A History of Child Abuse and Infanticide" in that collection. Pleck, *Domestic Tyranny* continues to be lucid and helpful for the late twentieth century as well as for earlier periods. There have been numerous studies of child abuse since World War II. Among them, David C. Gil, *Violence against Children: Physical Child Abuse in the United States* (Cambridge, Mass.: Harvard University Press, 1970) stands out. Robert Mnookin provides a critical review of policy in "Foster Care—In Whose Best Interest?" *Harvard Educational Review* 43 (November 1973). A more recent analysis of the rates of child abuse (and of the kinds of child abuse reported) is Alene Byer Russell and Cynthia Trainor, *Trends in Child Abuse and Neglect: A National Perspective* (Denver: American Humane Association, 1984). A recent criticism of current child abuse reporting policies is Douglas J. Basharov, "Unfounded Allegations—A New Child Abuse Problem," *Public Interest* 83 (Spring 1986).

The best treatment of the history of the juvenile court is Ryerson, *The Best-Laid Plans*. For very recent developments, Ryerson may be supplemented with Peter S. Prescott, *The Child Savers: Juvenile Justice Observed* (New York: Alfred A. Knopf, 1981), which provides a compelling inside look at the juvenile justice system in the city of New York. Sutton, *Stubborn Children* is also useful for its discussion of the workings of the juvenile justice system.

The effort to use litigation to win rights for handicapped children can be followed in Donald N. Bersoff, "From Courthouse to Schoolhouse: Using the Legal System to Secure the Right to an Appropriate Education," *American Journal of Orthopsychiatry* 52 (July 1982), and Peter B. Edelman, "The Massachusetts Task Force Reports: Advocacy for Children," *Harvard Educational Review* 43 (November 1973). For a conservative critique of the process, see John C. Pittenger and Peter Kuriloff, "Educating the Handicapped in Reforming a Radical Law," *Public Interest* 66 (Winter 1982).

On the question of the usefulness of litigation for children, see Robert H. Mnookin, *In the Interest of Children: Advocacy Law Reform and Public Policy* (San Francisco: W. H. Freeman and Co., 1985), and a review of that work by Gary B. Melton, "Litigation *In the Interest of Children*," *Law and Human Behavior* 10 (December 1986). Continuing efforts on behalf of children's rights by the American Civil Liberties Union are described in "Victims of Child Welfare: A Proposal for Funding" and in the case summaries available from the Children's Rights Project of the ACLU. On the efforts of the ACLU, see also Marcia Lowry, "Derring-do in the 1980s: Child Welfare Impact Legislation after the Warren Years," *Family Law Quarterly* 20 (Summer 1986). For an assessment of the difficulties of legislation during the years of the Burger Court, see Nat Stern, "The Burger Court and the Diminishing Constitutional Rights of Minors: A Brief Overview," *Arizona State Law Review* 50 (November 1985).

The issue of special advocates for children is described in Donald N.

Duquette and Sarah H. Ramsey, "Representation of Children in Child Abuse and Neglect Cases: An Empirical Look at What Constitutes Effective Representation," *University of Michigan Journal of Law Reform* 20 (Winter 1987). On the impact of *In re Gault* on juvenile court procedure, see Henry H. Foster, Jr. and Doris Jonas Freed, "A Bill of Rights for Children," *Family Law Quarterly* 6 (Winter 1972), and Gail Marker and Paul R. Friedman, "Re-Thinking Children's Rights," *Children Today* 2 (November–December 1973).

The literature on active advocacy on behalf of children in the 1970s is immense. See, for example, David Gottlieb, ed., *Children's Liberation* (Englewood Cliffs, N.J.: Prentice-Hall, 1973); Beatrice and Ronald Gross, eds., *The Children's Rights Movement: Overcoming the Oppression of Young People* (Garden City, N.Y.: Anchor Books, 1977); Advisory Committee on Child Development, Assembly of Behavioral and Social Sciences, National Research Council, *Toward a National Policy for Children and Families* (Washington, D.C.: National Academy of Sciences, 1977); Kenneth Keniston and the Carnegie Council on Children, *All Our Children: The American Family under Pressure* (New York: Harcourt Brace Jovanovich, 1977); and Kenneth Wooden, *Weeping in the Playtime of Others: America's Incarcerated Children* (New York: McGraw-Hill, 1976). Among the more prominent child liberationists are Richard Farson, whose *Birthrights* (New York: Macmillan, 1974) is a basic text of this position, and John Holt (*Escape from Childhood* [New York: Ballantine Books, 1974]). Also of this persuasion is Howard Cohen, *Equal Rights for Children* (Totowa, N.J.: Littlefield, Adams & Co., 1980). Neal Postman, *The Disappearance of Childhood* (New York: Delacorte Press, 1982) provides vigorous opposition to the child liberationist view.

The best way to understand the position of the Children's Defense Fund is to study its publications, of which *A Call for Action to Make Our Nation Safe for Children: A Briefing Book on the State of American Children in 1988* (Washington, D.C.: Children's Defense Fund, 1988) is representative. Interviews with both Marian Wright Edelman (founder of the CDF) and Justine Wise Polier (distinguished retired juvenile court judge and an officer of the CDF) can be found in *Harvard Educational Review* 44 (February 1974).

Index

The Author

Joseph M. Hawes is professor of history at Memphis State University, where he teaches courses in the history of American childhood and the American family. He is the author of *Children in Urban Society* (1971) and the co-editor of *American Childhood* (1985), *Growing Up in America* (1985), and the forthcoming *American Families* and *Children in International Historical Perspective.* Currently at work on a history of American children and youth in the 1920s, Hawes is co-editor (with N. Ray Hiner) of Twayne's History of American Childhood Series.

9336

DATE DUE		
OCT 21 1999		
	DATE DUE	
MAY 1 4 1993		